Victim/Victor: It's Your Choice

A Healing Journey Through the Psalms

B. Kay Coulter

Edited by Janet K. Crews

Victim/Victor: It's Your Choice
by B. Kay Coulter
Edited by Janet K. Crews

Printed in the United States of America

Library of Congress Control Number: 2002107750
ISBN 1-591601-31-2

Xulon Press
11350 Random Hills Road
Suite 800
Fairfax, VA 22030
(703) 279-6511
XulonPress.com

To order additional copies, call 1-866-909-BOOK (2665).

God bless your own journey.

B. Kay Coulter

Is. 26:3

Acknowledgments

I want to express my deepest gratitude to friends Tony, Guyann, Christen, Ramona, and Betty for being volunteer readers of this book while it was in the process of becoming. Your notes and insights were invaluable to me. Also, my thanks go to those who have shared their stories with me so they can be an encouragement to others. My very special thanks to my friend and ministry partner Janet Crews for her many hours of editing work. Without the help of all these friends this book would not have come into being. It is my prayer that through this book many will look to God for the healing that is needed in their lives.

This book is dedicated to:

My children Grace, Paul, and Peter
and my grandchildren Lauren, Luke, and Joel.
May God's blessings be upon them and the
generations of children that follow them.

Contents

Introduction 11

1. Waiting for Applause 15
2. A Widespread Problem 21
3. A Legacy of Abuse 29
4. Portrait of a Victim 41
5. Poison: Fear 49
6. Journey from Fear to Faith 53
7. A Sure Foundation 71
8. The Paths of Righteousness 81
9. Poison: Anger 87
10. From Bondage to Freedom 95
11. Poison: Bitterness 111
12. From Bitterness to Joy 119
13. Plight of the Abuser 133
14. Pathway to Healing 155
15. Breaking the Cycle 173
16. Victors' Hall of Fame 199

Notes 225

Introduction

There could be several reasons why you are reading this book. Perhaps you are being or have been victimized in the past and are having difficulty healing from the injury. Your desire is to know how you can experience victory over past hurts. Perhaps you know others who are in bondage and you would like to help them experience freedom. I believe this book can be of help to both kinds of readers.

Within these pages, you will see portraits of victims and victimizers. According to *Webster's New World Dictionary*, a victim is "someone or something killed, destroyed, injured, or otherwise harmed by, or suffering from, some act, condition, agency, or circumstance." We will explore what constitutes a victim, how a victim can break loose from a victim mentality and what it means to live victoriously.

Not only will you learn how to be healed from hurts of the past, but you will also learn how to break the cycle of hurtful family experiences that are passed to succeeding generations. You will learn what follows personal healing and you will read the stories of others who have overcome their pasts.

In American culture today, there are many who tell us that we are victims—victims of physical abuse, harassment, discrimination, and circumstances in general. Sometimes this word is overused. How willingly we have adopted these victim labels for ourselves, using them as excuses for not being personally responsible for our actions. The problem is even prevalent among Christians. Christians, of all people, should be free from these labels. We have a message of hope and encouragement to give to others because Christ has set us free.

Freedom is realized when we are no longer bound to fearful and angry responses. It has been my observation that people respond to abuse with either fear or anger, and they often allow these responses to determine a lifelong mindset. Either mindset becomes bondage and prevents healing.

While it is true that many have been victimized, I contend that it is not necessary for us to continue to live as victims. We have a choice. We can choose what our response to victimization is going to be. Let us explore together our options as we see ourselves from God's perspective. God has provided for us an escape from this bondage. He knows that we can live free and victorious lives.

Christians have a message of hope to give to a hurting, dying world of victims. How can we deliver this message of hope if we do not demonstrate it in our own lives? We need to wake up to the fact that if we do not deal with issues of bondage in our own lives, we will pass on to the next generation much of the same abuse that was passed down to us.

I believe the Bible speaks both to the victim and to the victimizer in matters of abuse. I believe it also speaks to the issue of generational sin—habitual abuse that is passed on. As Christians, we not only have the power to live victoriously, but we also have the responsibility to break the cycle of generational sin in our families.

I have come to these conclusions based upon my own personal experiences, my interaction with others, and my lifelong study of God's Word. My own response to victimization was fear. God has delivered me from bondage to fear, and I know He will free others who will turn to Him. The poems interspersed throughout are some of my original songs that I wrote out of my own experiences.

In this book, you will learn from many sources, including theologians, Christian counselors, psychologists, therapists, and the stories of real people with real problems. Most of all, you will learn God's perspective from the many Scriptures that are shared. Though both the Old and New Testaments speak to the issue of victimization and generational abuse, my primary Scriptural source is the Psalms.

It is my prayer that every reader will gain new insights into how to deal with the problem of victimization. It is also my prayer that each reader will be edified and better equipped to help others.

Treasure of Heaven

By B. Kay Coulter

Jesus loves the children.
We must love them, too.
For they're treasures from Heaven
Sent to me and you.
Treasure of Heaven
Sent into our lives.
A priceless gift of love to us
As seen in God's eyes.
A helpless little bundle
Placed within our care.
An angel sent from Heaven;
An answer to our prayer.
No baby is unwanted.
Every one is loved.
For each child is created
By a loving God above.
Treasure of Heaven
Sent into our lives.
A priceless gift of love to us
As seen in God's eyes.

CHAPTER ONE

Waiting for Applause

The stage was set! The child actress/singer entered, ready to deliver a memorable performance. Her naturally curly hair bounced with her every step as she took her place on the makeshift platform. She was just five years old, with a sprinkling of freckles adorning her face and a smile that would brighten any dreary room. She began to sing, not just with her voice, but also with her heart. It seemed she was born for the stage. She sang and then waited for the expected applause, but the room was silent, vacant of any audience.

You see, the platform was not a Hollywood stage, nor was the child a professional. She was not a star, for her performance took place in the privacy of her childhood home. Naturally a happy-go-lucky child, she spent many hours in the world of her imagination. Pretending was her favorite pastime—pretending to be a princess or movie star, or a famous singer or dancer. In her imaginary world, she could express herself freely with all the creativity that a five-year-old could muster. In this world, everyone loved her and she felt important and valuable. By all appearances, it seemed that all was well.

Part of her pretending took her to an imaginary stage—

actually the hearth in front of the fireplace. Of course, her mind conjured an audience for her performance. What did a five-year-old perform? Her repertoire mainly consisted of hymns and songs learned at church, such as "Trust and Obey."

> When we walk with the Lord
> In the light of His Word
> What a glory He sheds on our way!
> When we do His good will;
> He abides with us still,
> And with all who will trust and obey.
> Trust and obey, for there's no other way
> To be happy in Jesus but to trust and obey.*

Even at this early age, she had a sense of the presence of God as Father, thus she knew the One of whom she sang. He served as audience—the audience of One in the absence of a human audience.

The words to that particular hymn, "Trust and Obey," would become very significant in the girl's journey into adulthood. Her very nature was one of childlike trust and a desire to please others, and it was those principles of trust and obedience that would eventually lead her to be an overcomer. She would have much to overcome.

Indeed, the truths expressed in this song would be needed for a lifetime, for it was only in her imaginary world that she felt loved and wanted. In her real world, all was not well. From an early age, however, this child would put in place a strong denial system that would prevent her from acknowledging outwardly that anything was wrong. Inside herself, however, she knew her real world was not what she wanted it to be.

---

* From *The Baptist Hymnal* (Nashville, Tennessee: Convention Press, 1991, #447)

Inwardly, she longed for an audience of real people—namely her family— who would applaud her and affirm that she had worth and beauty and talent. She longed to know that she was special and cherished. She had had a small taste of that "special" feeling in her very early years, but that feeling would be obliterated by later rejection, neglect, and abuse. Somehow she always had the feeling she had not been wanted in the family, and the neglect and abuse of her father confirmed this in her heart. At the tender young age of six she began to suffer the effects of molestation, verbal abuse, and emotional neglect.

I am well acquainted with the little girl depicted in the scene above, for I played the leading role in this real-life drama. As I think back on my childhood, I try to bring into focus not only the actual memories, but also the words of other family members who have talked about it. It has been over a period of fourteen years in my adult life that I have been able to assemble the pieces of the puzzle that make up who I am. Finally, the past begins to take shape in my mind's eye.

My reflections take me to when I was three years old. My family lived in town where neighbors were in close proximity to one another. I was the youngest child in my family and six years younger than my next-in-line sister. I was made very aware that I was the baby of the family, and sometimes I did not feel good about this. On several occasions, my mother would need a baby-sitter and would ask our across-the-street neighbor to keep me. On at least one of these occasions, my mother's trust in the reliability of our neighbors was betrayed. It was one of those times when my mother left me with the neighbors that something happened that has had negative repercussions for many years. For as I was left this particular day, the man of that family happened to be home. Mr. W was a heavy drinker and became quite abusive under the influence of alcohol. When I began to search my childhood memories, in my mind's eye, I watched this scene unfold as if I were looking through prison bars. I found out much later that these were bars on a crib. I remember feeling resentful about having to nap in a crib. After all, I was all of three years old, and I thought I was too big to sleep in a baby bed! As it turned out, the baby bed did actually become prison-like, as I was at the mercy of a grown-up man who picked me up, leered at me, and proceeded to molest me. He must have been drinking, because when I think of this episode of abuse, I can almost smell the liquor. To this day, I have a great aversion to liquor of any kind, including its smell. Other feelings that I had to deal with in the days ahead were fear and a sense of helplessness. I can remember begging my mother not to make me go to that house again. Of course, I couldn't express the reasons for my fear and distress, so no one ever knew what had taken place there. In my child's mind, the sense of betrayal was overwhelming, so I blotted the episode out of my memory for many years. I believe the blocking of this memory from my mind was God's grace at work, for a young child is not equipped to deal with the enormity of such sin. In His graciousness God allowed me to mature to the point where I could deal with it before it was revealed to me. It was only as an adult that I could see the truth of 1 Corinthians 4:5: "He will bring to light the things of darkness."

God brought the former things of darkness to light for me as I came to Him for healing. I will share more of this healing process in the pages of this book. Today I can say I am free from the bondage of past hurts, and I desire that others be free as well.

The abuse I suffered had the potential to be passed on to my children. In many cases, this is the natural outcome of one who has been victimized. I can praise God, however, that many of the devastating effects of generational abuse were avoided in the connection between my children and me. Why is this? I believe that there are several reasons my children have escaped this legacy of abuse. One reason is that God brought about an emotional healing in me when my children were still young. A second reason is that my husband and I committed ourselves early in marriage to following God's plan for our lives. We made a choice and that choice has made all the difference for my children and grandchildren.

This book is about choices. Each of us make choices every day—some of which have little lasting significance, some of which have great significance and have far-reaching consequences.

CHAPTER TWO

A Widespread Problem

My story of abuse is not a unique one. I represent millions of victims of childhood abuse. This matter of victimization is a popular topic and has been addressed by many people, both within and without the church. Sexual abuse, especially, is a much-discussed subject. Attention to this area of abuse was demonstrated at a seminar that I recently attended. This seminar was sponsored by several large churches of a mainline denomination and was held in Houston, Texas. One of the seminars offered to participants was "Hot Topics in the Church." In attending this conference, I learned that one of the issues that is being addressed by leading decision-makers within this denomination is the church's view of sexuality. A specific issue at hand was whether or not to ordain homosexuals or allow them in places of leadership. This denomination is struggling with how to develop a policy that will fit their interpretation of Scripture.

One's view of sexuality is, and historically has been, a volatile issue that impacts many aspects of life. The Church is not the only part of culture that is grappling with this issue. There is much in the news about sexual misconduct, sexual crimes, and abuse. Some headline samples taken from recently published local newspapers are:

- Straying husbands, lovers spread cervical cancer
- Lawyer tries to aid abused children
- Children and Sexual Behavior
- Teenager faces sentencing for impregnating girlfriend
- Reader: girls are not only ones molested (from an Ann Landers column)

In addition to this small sampling of headlines, there are many who have written on the subject of abuse in the media and in literature:

> Statistics show that the majority of clients who seek help for chemical addictions are victims of sexual abuse. In 1989, 2.4 million acts of sexual abuse were reported, according to U.S. Department of Justice. Addiction follows abuse, because the abusive event causes pain and the alcohol, drugs or sex help the victim mask the injury.[1]

> Statistics indicate that thirty-four million women in the United States are victims of child sexual abuse. It is estimated that a child is molested every two minutes.[2]

A recent *Los Angeles Times* poll showed that nearly one out of every four people in the United States had been molested during childhood; and that for every victim known, nine are hidden.[3] The same poll revealed that one in three victims had never told anyone about being molested. Statistics indicate that seventy-five percent of the children who have been victimized within the home have mothers who were victims as children.[4]

David Peters, a well-known expert in this area, stated on a recent radio program that he believes as high as seventy percent of women have no conscious awareness of a molestation that occurred in their pasts.[5] A Minneapolis survey of teenage prostitutes indicated seventy-five percent of them had been molested as children.[6] In his book, *Understanding Your Past—the Key to Your Future,* Dr. Cecil Osborne writes, "Feelings do not age. Feelings about past events are in us now. Time does not diminish childhood hurts . . . They do not erode or disappear."[7] One treatment center for child abuse has found consistently that:

> More than eighty percent of the mothers in the program have a background of sexual abuse. Some victims can trace sexual abuse to their mothers and even their grandmothers, making a legacy of four generations of sexual victimization.[8]

According to a study done by the Justice Department's Bureau of Justice Statistics:

> ...forty-eight percent of female inmates and 13 percent of jailed men have been abused sexually or physically at least once in their lives.... More than a quarter of the women—27 percent—and 3 percent of men said the abuse included rape. "The tragedy is that people who have been victimized often become victimizers themselves," said Eric E. Sterling, president of the Washington-based Criminal Justice Policy Foundation. "It's a cycle we could break, but it involves some expense. As a society, we haven't put our resources there."[9]

The conclusion of a study by Dr. Keerti V. Shah, Professor at the Johns Hopkins University School of Medicine, found "women are five to eleven times more likely to develop cervical cancer if their men frequent prostitutes or have many sexual partners."

> In the last 20 years, the suicide rate of children ages five to fourteen has more than doubled. It is now the sixth leading cause of death. Low self-esteem is not only a major contributor to death but also to disability.[10]

What do these statistics tell us about our society today? It would seem that there is a problem of epidemic proportions. What can be done about it? Is there any hope of reversing these trends? How can abuse—verbal, physical, emotional, and sexual—be stopped? How can we break the cycle of abuse so that it won't be passed down to future generations?

First of all, we can call it what it is: SIN! Acting out in abusive behavior is not a disease or something that a person cannot control. Abusive behavior happens because a person *chooses* to act in this manner. Indeed, abuse *is* sin and in recognizing this fact, we can begin to get the help we really need. Many may consider "sin" to be an old-fashioned word in our "enlightened age," but no thinking person can truly deny its existence. Dr. Henry Brandt says in his book, *The Heart of the Problem*:

> In my studies in clinical psychology, we grappled with the challenges of helping disturbed people...the hostile, hateful, resentful, rebellious, frustrated, confused, angry, cruel, selfish, dishonest, destructive people. We all agreed that these words accurately described the dark side of human behavior. We were taught that a person is a biological organism whose total personality is the product of functioning in a social and cultural context. What in the world can be changed or given to release this person from a prison of destructive emo-

> tions and behavior? "No deity can save us. We must save ourselves."
>
> This is the position taken in secular colleges, secular textbooks, in most graduate training, and in a formidable mass of "scientific research." This is the operating philosophy of government, heavily financed mental health agencies, professionally trained counselors, and the bulk of medically trained personnel. We spend billions of dollars annually searching for solutions.
>
> A massive group of people—intelligent, educated, influential, politically powerful people—who have the best interests of humanity at heart, firmly and fiercely reject the concept of sin, a creator, and a God. You might compare that host of people to a huge giant called Goliath. They firmly believe: God isn't. We are born with sinful hearts. Society only brings out of our hearts what is already there.[11]

This quote from Dr. Brandt very clearly shows what our society says to victims of abuse. It seems to me that worldly philosophies of dealing with bad behavior are quite inadequate. Wouldn't it be better to look to our Creator for guidance on this issue? Does the Bible speak to the sin of abuse? How should the Christian respond? I contend that the Word of God has much to say on this subject.

In our society, the evidence is ample that the principle of generational sin is at work, especially in the area of abuse. We know that many perpetrators come from dysfunctional families and carry out the same kind of abuse on their children which they received from their parents. The Bible has numerous examples of generational sin as well. A few examples from the Old Testament are:

- the sin of lying found in the lives of Abraham, Isaac, and Jacob (Genesis 12:13; 26:7; 27:1-46);

- the case from 1 Samuel 2:12-17, 22-25, 27-36 of Eli's failing "to restrain" his sons, and since he was also a primary model in Samuel's life, we see Samuel's repetition of this negative behavior in the lives of his own sons (1 Samuel 8:1-3);

- sexual immorality as exhibited in the lives of David and Solomon, father and son (2 Samuel 11-12; I Kings 11:1, 9).

Modern-day therapists deal with the catastrophic consequences of abuse passed from one generation to another as they see the wrecked lives of hurting people every day. One such therapist states:

> The dysfunctional patterns of communication, the degree to which the family is a "closed system," and the family's inability to resolve conflicts in a healthy way are all contributory factors that either allow for or reduce dysfunction in the following generation.[12]

Modern-day therapists are dealing with issues that were revealed in the Bible many centuries ago. Indeed, the Bible has much to say about the fact of generational sin. This fact is also very much in evidence in our culture. Let's bring it even closer to home. Is this truth evident in your family of origin? I know it is in mine. I also see the evidence of generational sin in people that I have observed for many years.

To demonstrate this truth of how a sin can be passed down to succeeding generations, let us examine the family

tree of a particular family—we'll call them the Andrewses.*
We will see in this family evidence of the legacy of generational sin. In this particular family, the sin that was passed on was sexual sin, and it can be traced through five generations. We'll begin with a set of parents, Father and Mother Andrews.

We don't know for sure about the father's early childhood, but we know that the mother was molested when she was a young girl. She grew into adulthood with a very negative view of sex and carried this attitude all her life. Her attitude also influenced how she brought up her daughters. She saw sex as a duty to her husband, however, so she did produce four children from their union. It is in the lives of these children that the principle of generational sin is demonstrated. To this family were born Frances, Sam, David, and Bonnie. Let us look at the outcome of sexual abuse on the daughters of Mr. and Mrs. Andrews and one of the sons.

* Based on interview with family member
*Names have been changed to protect privacy

CHAPTER THREE

A Legacy of Abuse

High Hopes

Frances was the firstborn in her family. She was intelligent, artistic, and sensitive. She had a great need for quiet and solitude, which others perceived as a desire to be unsociable. Though her family was not wealthy or important in the community, she had a bright future ahead. She studied hard, excelled in academics, and learned to develop her artistic talents to the professional level. Although she had the promise of a bright future, a dark shadow crossed the sunlit path of her life. She became a victim of sexual abuse at the hands of a grandfather. This event would greatly impact on her future choices: choices in selection of mates; choices in relation to her belief in God; choices in attitude and behavior.

Diagram 1 shows the family tree of Frances and succeeding generations, listing each family member's response to sexual abuse. These family members generally had an anger response, and you can see the thread of anger running through the generations. As you can trace from the diagram, Frances's unresolved anger carried into her adulthood and she, along with her two abusive husbands, passed this on to their children.

It is often true that anger begets bitterness, an unforgiving spirit, rebelliousness, defensiveness, and irrational behavior. All of these characteristics can be observed in Frances's life. This kind of deeply inbred anger often leads to the victim's becoming a victimizer, perpetuating the abuse. In Frances's case anger turned inward became bitterness, and it continues to destroy her as a cancer would destroy the body. Anger turned outward often becomes rebellion, as we will see demonstrated in the life of the daughter in this family.

A well-known theologian and pastor, R.C. Sproul, states on one of his teaching videos: "One of the foundations of anger is disappointment."[13] Certainly, when a child is molested by a family member, there is great disappointment. An abused child arrives at adulthood as an emotional cripple, full of disappointment, anger and/or fear.

Diagram 1

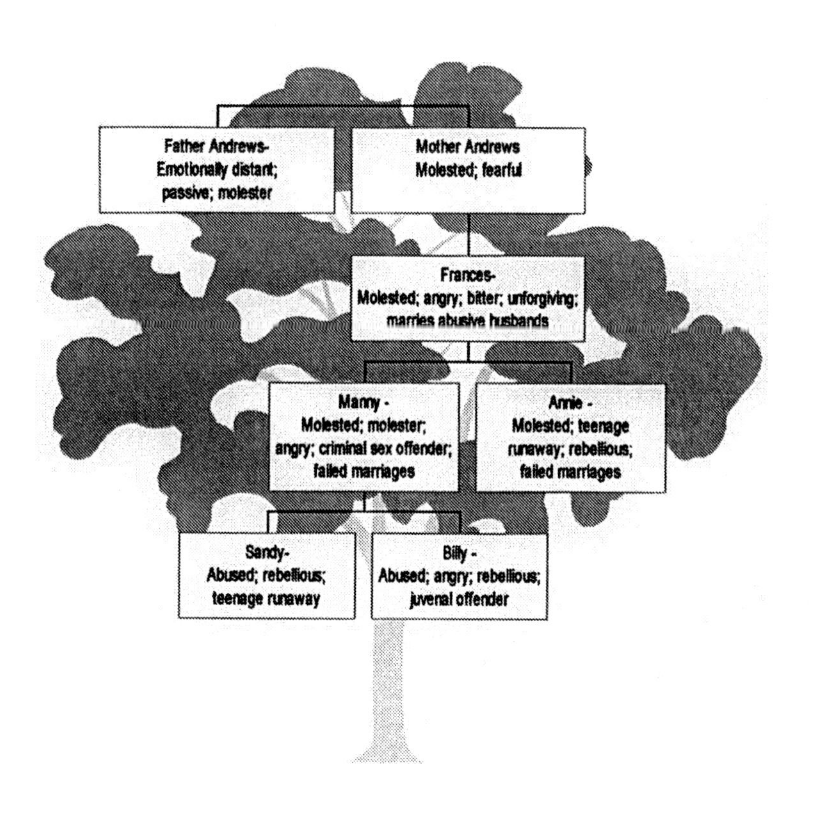
Father Andrews-
Emotionally distant;
passive; molester
Mother Andrews
Molested; fearful
Frances-
Molested; angry; bitter; unforgiving;
marries abusive husbands
Manny -
Molested; molester;
angry; criminal sex offender;
failed marriages
Annie -
Molested; teenage
runaway; rebellious;
failed marriages
Sandy-
Abused; rebellious;
teenage runaway
Billy -
Abused; angry; rebellious;
juvenal offender

Looking for Love in All the Wrong Places

Another daughter in this same family is Bonnie. Bonnie grew up as a tomboy, following her older brothers around, wanting to participate in "boy" things. She was multitalented, with a flair for drama, writing, art, and music. Always popular in school, she excelled in academics, athletics, and sociability. She was also a born leader and very strong-willed. However, her strong will did not protect her from being raped at age eight by a neighbor, and being molested repeatedly by her brothers. She was tough, though, and never told anyone, choosing to keep the sordid facts of the abuse to herself. How these violent acts against her affected her would be evinced over many years to come.

Diagram 2 shows her family tree and how a rebellious attitude arose from her anger response to childhood abuse. Bonnie was molested many times by her brothers, was rejected by her father, and taught by her mother that sex is bad. Under those circumstances, it was difficult for her to have a very good self-esteem. Since she felt unloved by her father, she sought to fill that void in her life by giving herself to other men. She was extremely in need of love and yet very angry about the wrong kind of "love" attention that had been given her. This led to a long period of rebellion, resulting in unfaithfulness, divorce, alienation from the church, and dabbling with the occult. Needless to say, this rebellious attitude greatly influenced the way she reared her children.

The good news, however, is that in mid-life she did become convicted of her sin, came to God for forgiveness, and began to feel the love of her Heavenly Father. Now, she no longer has to seek love in all the wrong places. Her life has been changed by the One Who specializes in redeeming fallen mankind. Sadly, in some ways the change came too late in her life to have a significant impact on her children.

Diagram 2

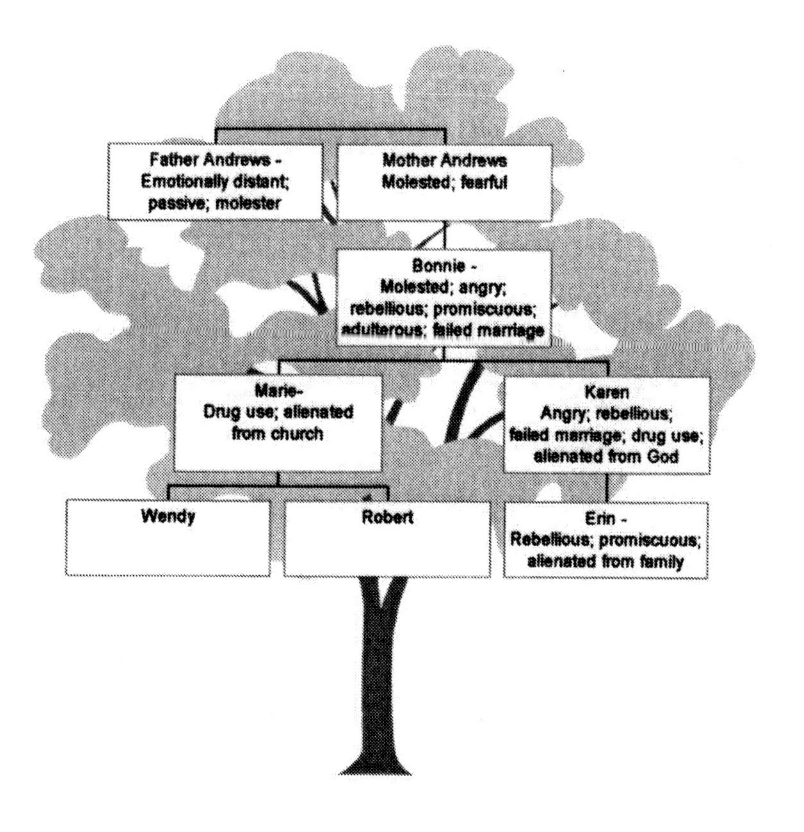
Father Andrews -
Emotionally distant;
passive; molester
Mother Andrews
Molested; fearful
Bonnie -
Molested; angry;
rebellious; promiscuous;
adulterous; failed marriage
Marie-
Drug use; alienated
from church
Karen
Angry; rebellious;
failed marriage; drug use;
alienated from God
Wendy
Robert
Erin -
Rebellious; promiscuous;
alienated from family

A Pattern of Abuse

Sam is the elder son in this very dysfunctional family. He started out in his high school years with a bright future in sports. Being a better-than-average football player qualified him to go to college on scholarship. All college plans were thwarted, however, by the fact that he found himself in the hapless position of unwanted fatherhood. His high school sweetheart had become pregnant and they hurriedly married in order to legitimize the birth of their first child.

Earlier in his teen years, Sam had been guilty of molesting his sister. Although he was not the instigator in the abuse, he did go along with it. It is not known what influenced him and his brother to believe that molesting a younger sister was acceptable. It is possible he was mimicking someone older and more experienced—perhaps his grandfather (who had molested his older sister). It is known that he suffered emotional neglect from his father and learned that females in this family were devalued.

Sam had a passive personality and adopted denial as a way of life. Because of his tendency to avoid controversy, he set in motion a chain of events that reached far into his future. The girl that he married in order to legitimize the child she carried also came from a dysfunctional family. She later bore three other children to Sam.

Diagram 3

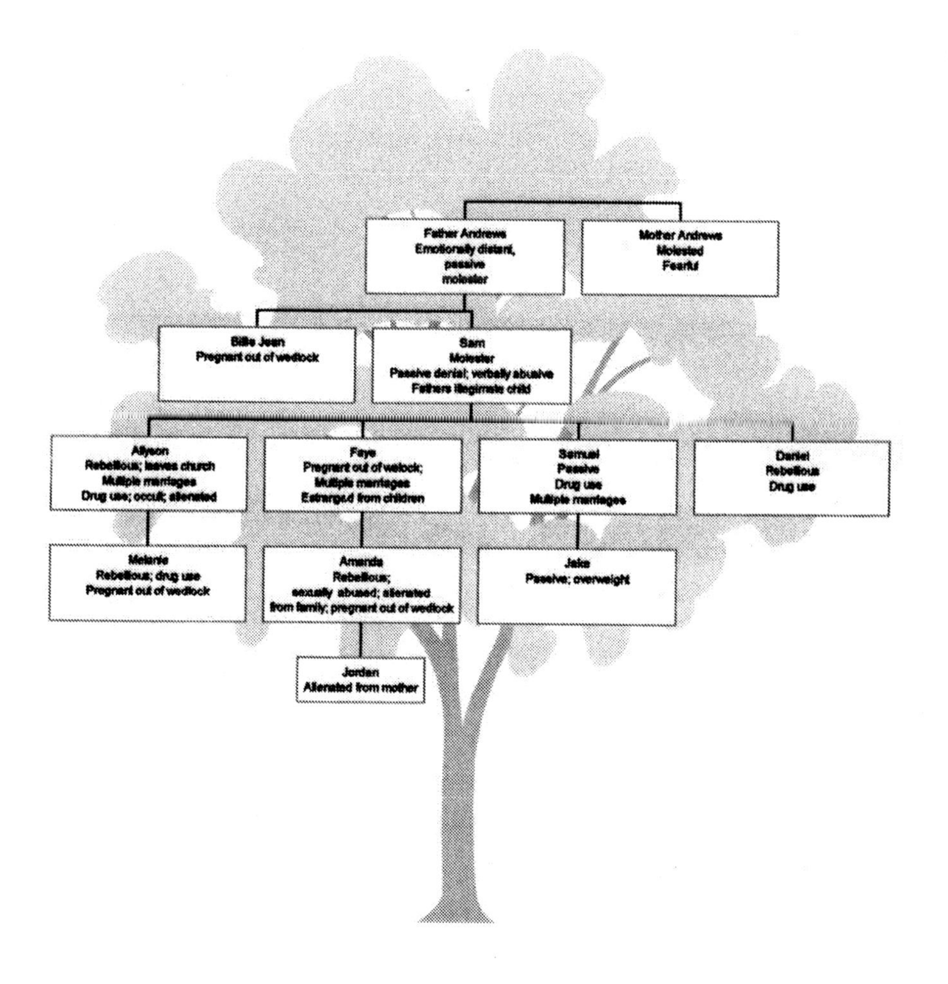
Father Andrews
Emotionally distant,
passive
molester
Mother Andrews
Molested
Fearful
Billie Jean
Pregnant out of wedlock
Sam
Molester
Passive denial; verbally abusive
Fathers illegimate child
Allyson
Rebellious; leaves church
Multiple marriages
Drug use; occult; alienated
Faye
Pregnant out of welock;
Multiple marriages
Estranged from children
Samuel
Passive
Drug use
Multiple marriages
Daniel
Rebellious
Drug use
Melanie
Rebellious; drug use
Pregnant out of wedlock
Amanda
Rebellious;
sexually abused; alienated
from family; pregnant out of wedlock
Jake
Passive; overweight
Jordan
Alienated from mother

They were erratic in their church attendance, and eventually turned away from the church of their upbringing. The firstborn, Allyson, repeated this mistake and turned away from the church in her teen years. Her decision proved to be a big mistake, because she began a journey of "self-discovery" that led her into drugs, multiple marriages, occult study, and alienation from the family. During her second marriage, Allyson had her only child, a daughter, Melanie. Allyson, in her spiral downward, rejected Melanie early in her life. In addition to the rejection by her mother, Melanie was torn between her estranged parents. Allyson spent many years trying to redeem that relationship. Even though Melanie's relationship with her mother was restored to some extent, the wounds of rejection crippled her; and she, like her mother, went her own way—looking for love! She hung out with the wrong crowd, was rebellious, and got involved in drugs. Before age twenty Melanie became pregnant out of wedlock and married the father of the baby. Allyson, after divorcing her third husband, is still searching for happiness and stability.

The stories of the other three children of Sam are similar, as you can see from Diagram 3. Every one of the children has brought much grief to his/her parents. This same grief has been passed down to their children and grandchildren. What a legacy! There is hope for each one, however, as they choose to break the cycle of abuse. One by one, the children are beginning to turn back to God. But, oh, how many wrecked lives could have been avoided if they had made the right choices sooner!

The Andrews children from the preceding stories all have something in common: a history of sexual abuse. In an analysis of the family histories of each, we can see an illustration of different responses to the same kind of abuse.

We can see the very destructive "sap" of anger running through the branches of the family trees of Frances and

Bonnie. This anger produced badly damaged fruit. For Sam, however, another destructive force was at work—that of fear (which led to his passivity and denial).

I think it is apparent in human experience that the principle of generational sin is at work. Also, the Bible addresses this principle emphatically in its admonitions to God's people. One of the Ten Commandments states:

> You shall not bow down to them or worship them; for I, the LORD your God, am a jealous God, punishing the children for the sin of the fathers to the third and fourth generation of those who hate me, but showing love to a thousand generations of those who love me and keep my commandments (Exodus 20:5 KJV).

2 Chronicles 30:7-9 warns the Jews to avoid sinning as their forefathers had done:

> Do not be like your fathers and brothers who sinned against the LORD God of their fathers and were destroyed. Do not be stubborn, as they were, but yield yourselves to the LORD and come to his temple which He has sanctified for ever, and worship the LORD your God so that his fierce anger will turn away from you. For if you turn to the LORD again, your brothers and your children will be treated mercifully by their captors, and they will not continue to turn away His face from you if you return to Him.

The New Testament gives us this warning from Ephesians 6:4: "Fathers, do not exasperate your children; instead bring them up in the training and instruction of the Lord." The concept of generational sin and particularly the principle of God's "visiting the iniquity of the fathers upon the children" captured my attention and is a backdrop to my study of how the Psalms speak to the abused and the abuser.

At first glance this judgmental action on the part of God may seem too severe, or at the very least, unfair. What exactly does this mean? Does it mean that God puts a curse on succeeding generations of innocent children because of the sins of their forebears? Why should an "innocent" child have to suffer for the sins of his parents? A better question might be: Are there natural consequences to sinful behavior that spill over into succeeding generations? These are hard questions and require thought and prayer. I think the answer lies in a broader reading of Scripture, and not in taking one out of context and building a doctrine on it. For example, if we read the verse following Exodus 20:5, we can receive a broader picture of the character of God. Verse 6 reads, "And showing mercy unto thousands of them that love me, and keep my commandments."

What we see is a God who loves us and desires the best for us; therefore He has given us instructions by which to live. Sometimes these instructions come in directives, such as the Ten Commandments and many of Jesus' teachings. Sometimes they come in more subtle ways as we view the lives of real people who lived when the Bible was being written. The lessons we learn here can be applied universally, for human nature is the same whether it be in ancient times or modern times. We know that:

> The word of God is living and active. Sharper than any double-edged sword, it penetrates even to dividing soul and spirit, joints and marrow; it judges the thoughts and attitudes of the heart. Nothing in all creation is hidden from God's sight. Everything is uncovered and laid bare before the eyes of him to whom we must give account (Hebrews 4:12).

For the one who is seeking to know how to live life optimally—freed from the past, functioning in the present, and looking forward with faith to the future—the Bible offers the answers. So, let us begin our journey into the Psalms and see what is offered here that would free us from the chains of victimization.

Free to Be

By B. Kay Coulter

Free to be,
Free to be me,
Free to be the me God created me to be.
Free to do,
Free to go,
Free to know the God who loves me so.
Free to sing,
Free to praise all my days
The God Who delivered me.
Oh, yes I'm free.
You can be, too —
Free to love the God Who saves you.
I have come from a place of captivity;
My childhood innocence stolen from me.
And though I was victimized —I realize —
I can live in victory.
No longer bound by my sin;
Not my own or the sins of evil men.
Through forgiveness I can find—true peace of mind.
Yes, my soul is free within.
My fears no longer possess me;
No more chains of insecurity.
The healing has begun—for Christ has come
And has set me free indeed.

CHAPTER FOUR

Portrait of a Victim

Numerous books have been written on the subject of abuse, particularly sexual abuse, listing symptoms of victims and the struggles with which they contend. I believe that the Psalms give us methods of treatment for these symptoms that will ultimately lead to healing. Some of the symptoms evident in victims are listed below.

In Adults:

- Sense of betrayal
- Fear of abandonment
- Relational difficulties
- Lacking in confidence
- Withdrawal
- Makes poor life choices
- Low self-esteem
- Unexplained illness and disability
- Sexual promiscuity
- Sense of alienation
- Lack of trust
- Inability to communicate
- Irrational behavior
- Caught in the cycle of abuse
- Negative view of life
- Paranoia

In Children who have been sexually abused:[14]

Fear of specific persons or situations/strangers	Excessive washing/baths
Withdrawal (social or emotional)	Unprovoked crying spells
Clinging to significant adult	Fear of being alone
Refusal to go to school	
Changes in type of fantasy play	Early sexual precociousness
Loss of appetite	Running away
Personality change	Nightmares
Poor self-image/ low self-esteem	Bed wetting/change in sleep patterns

Note: One or even two of these symptoms are not indicative of sexual abuse. A combination of several (four or more) might indicate a need for concern.

> "Statistics show that the majority of clients who seek help for chemical addictions are victims of sexual abuse," said Douglas Weiss, a speaker at a recent Recovery Works Addiction Symposium held in Temple, Texas. He also stated that, "stages of psychosocial development—trust, autonomy, initiative, identity, intimacy and integrity—stop at the time the abuse takes place, and the counselor has to help the addict rebuild the steps that were missed.[15]

As one can see from the statistics in chapter one, the family trees in chapter two, and the symptom list above, our society is full of victims. The presence of dysfunctional families is becoming so common that often I am tempted to wonder if there is a "functional" family anywhere. This should not surprise us, considering that the very first family in history was dysfunctional. We know them as Adam, Eve, Cain, and Abel.

Every day we encounter victims—in our own experiences with others, or in learning about them through the media. We are told over and over that we (as a society) are victims. There are victims of crime, victims of spousal abuse, and victims of child abuse. We are told regularly that we are also victimized by...

- the government
- the environment
- the stock market
- law enforcement officials
- poverty
- poor education
- sexual harassment
- discrimination in the workplace
- and even the church.

The list could go on and on. Suffice it to say that we can view ourselves as a nation full of "victims." However, let us determine who really are victims. Although there may be some doubt as to some claims of victimization, I believe all would agree that sexual abuse is definitely one of the most prevalent forms of victimization.

Much has been written to inform us of how we are victims. This has led to an attitude of excuse-giving for our bad behavior. Even for particularly heinous crimes, we (society) accept excuses for the behavior of criminals. Because most abusers come out of abusive backgrounds (i.e., abused as children), we accept the rationale that they just couldn't help themselves when they perpetrated abuse on others. The thinking goes something like this: "You were sexually molested as a young boy, so of course your sense of sexuality is out of balance. This explains why you raped 25 women."

An interesting article caught my eye recently in my hometown paper. It contained the story of a romance novelist who had been accused of plagiarizing another well-known writer. Although she admitted to the "crime", she blamed her acts on a "psychological disorder." She states, "I recently learned that my essentially random and non-pervasive acts of copying are attributable to a psychological problem that I never even suspected I had."[16] In other words, she was just a victim of a chain of circumstances, therefore she should not have to be accountable for her behavior.

Even in less extreme cases where no crime is committed, we find ourselves excusing bad behavior. We even fool ourselves into thinking we somehow have a constitutional right to act any way we choose, without regard to how our behavior impacts others. In the following editorial written by George F. Will of the *Washington Post*, he titles his column "ADA affording rights to the obnoxious?" and states:

> Compassionate government has recently rained new rights and entitlements so rapidly that you may have missed this beauty: You have a right to be a colossally obnoxious jerk on the job. If you are just slightly offensive, your right will not kick in. But if you are seriously insufferable to colleagues at work, you have a right not to be fired, and you are entitled to have your employer make reasonable accommodations for your "disability." That is how the Americans with Disabilities Act of 1990 (ADA) is being construed. Consider the Diagnostic and Statistical Manual of Mental Disorders' (DSM) definition of "oppositional defiant disorder" as a pattern of "negativistic, defiant, disobedient and hostile behavior toward authority figures." Diagnostic criteria include "often loses temper," "often deliberately annoys people," "is often touchy" or "spiteful or vindictive." The DSM's list of "personality disorders" includes "anti-social personality disorder "('a pervasive pattern of disregard for...the rights of

> others...callous, cynical...and inflated and arrogant self-appraisal'); histrionic personality disorder" ('excessive emotionality and attention-seeking...inappropriately sexually provocative or seductive'); "narcissistic personality disorder" ('grandiosity, need for admiration... boastful and pretentious...interpersonally exploitative...may assume that they do not have to wait in line'); "avoidant personality disorder" ('social inhibition, feelings of inadequacy'); "dependent personality disorder" ('submissive and clinging behavior'); "obsessive-compulsive personality disorder" ('preoccupation with orderliness, perfectionism...may be excessively conscientious, scrupulous...mercilessly self-critical...rigidly deferential to authority'). It is momentous...for society to decide that what once were considered faults of mind and flaws of character are "personality disorders" akin to physical disabilities that demand legal accommodation.[17]

G.E. Zuriff, professor of psychology at Wheaton College and a clinical psychologist at MIT, says in his essay "Medicalizing Character" that "people manifesting these traits should be held morally responsible for them. They should be encouraged to accommodate to society rather than the reverse." I agree with Mr. Zuriff.

With such a proliferation of victimization and such a propensity for excuse-making, how can we determine who the true victims are and how can they be helped to overcome a "victim" attitude? My contention is that even though I may have been victimized, I do not have to live like a victim. Instead, I can be a victor. This can happen because of the choices I make.

Psalm 37, in particular, speaks to me emphatically about the problem of victimization. King David wrote of his fears that rose out of his own victimization. He had been wrongly persecuted by King Saul, even to the point of fleeing for his life. He says in Psalm 40:12, "For troubles without number surround me," and "my heart fails within me." Verse 14 of the same Psalm tells us that David prayed that "those who seek to take my life be put to shame and confusion...."

As I see it, David's primary response to being victimized was fear. Fear rises out of insecurity, based upon past disappointments. The outcome of a fear-based response will be feelings of inadequacy, inferiority, and lack of self-worth. There is another possible response that is also brought out in Psalms—that of anger. There were times when David's anger toward his enemies showed. Psalm 35 makes this clear in verses 1, 4-6:

> Contend, O LORD, with those who
>   contend with me;
> fight against those who fight against
>   me!
> May those who seek my life
> be disgraced and put to shame;
> may those who plot my ruin
> be turned back in dismay.
>
> May they be like chaff before the
>   wind,
> with the angel of the LORD driving
>   them away;
> may their path be dark and slippery,
>   with the angel of the LORD pursuing
>   them.

Psalms is not merely words flowing from the pen of someone in an ivory tower. Rather, it is a divinely inspired diary, with David's life serving as a mural painted upon history, through which we can see God's teaching. David had to live the truth before he could teach it to others.

Two primary responses on the part of victims stand out to

me in these verses—the responses of FEAR and ANGER, or sometimes a combination of both. I believe that most of the other symptoms on the previous victim list arise out of these two responses. The Psalms not only present the potentially toxic effects of fear and anger, but also give us antidotes that will lead to healing. I am not speaking of the fear and anger that a victim feels initially, for these emotions are natural and expected. Rather, I am speaking to those who have been victimized in the past, and long after the abusive act has taken place, choose a lifestyle that is characterized by fear or anger. Let us examine under the microscope of God's Word the poisonous effects of such a lifestyle to discover what actually takes place in the mind of the victim.

CHAPTER FIVE

Poison: Fear

First I would like to examine the fear response. There is a natural fear instinct built into humans. We become afraid when we feel threatened, which leads to the *flight or fight* response. Dr. Norman Vincent Peale defines two kinds of fear in his little book entitled, *How to Handle Tough Times*: "Normal fear is necessary for our protection and for the exercise of a sensible caution. But abnormal fear is something altogether different."

In addition to natural fear, we also must recognize that there is a fear that we should have in our attitude toward God. To fear God is to reverence Him. We recognize His sovereignty in the affairs of men, and we acknowledge that He is all-knowing and all-powerful. The Scriptures promise us that if we have a reverent attitude toward God, then we will be the recipients of a great treasure.

> He will be the sure foundation for your
> times,
> a rich store of salvation and wisdom
> and knowledge;
> the fear of the LORD is the key to
> this treasure. (Isaiah 33:6)

> Praise the LORD.
> Blessed is the man who fears the
> LORD,
> who finds great delight in his
> commands. (Psalm 112:1)

In referring to fear as a poison, I am not talking about natural, healthy fear or the fear (reverence) that we give to God. Rather, I am referring to a response that leads to a fearful lifestyle. This kind of fear becomes a mindset and influences our thoughts, attitudes, and actions. A fearful mindset rises out of insecurity, based upon past disappointments. The outcome of a fear-based response will be feelings of inadequacy, inferiority and low self-esteem, lack of trust, paranoia, and a sense of abandonment.

John Powell, in his book, *Why Am I Afraid to Tell You Who I Am?,* highlights one reason for fear in the heart of a victim. The words are from a real person who came to him for counseling. The answer this person gave was, "I am afraid to tell you who I am, because, if I tell you who I am, you may not like who I am, and it's all that I have." The answer "reflects something of the imprisoning fears and self-doubt which cripple most of us and keep us from forward movement on the road to maturity, happiness, and true love."

As a victim myself whose primary response to abuse was fear, I can tell you what it is like to live in fear. For the most part I have overcome the tendency to respond to hurtful situations with fear, but I recently had an experience that reminded me that I must be ever vigilant in this area of my life. I found myself in the situation of possibly losing my best friend. I could see that she was being led into a very destructive relationship, but unfortunately we were not in agreement about this. The situation became very intense as we tried to work through it, and I became depressed and fearful. For a period of weeks I lapsed into my old habit of fearfulness and worry. As I began to come out of this fearful time, I felt impressed that I should journalize about what I had just experienced. I would like to share with you my experiences and what I learned from them.

What is it like to live in fear? When one gives in to fear, it is as if fear takes control, taking on a life of its own. We have heard the phrase "fear gripped my heart." This phrase is a very graphic description of what actually takes place physically. There is actual physical pain caused from a tightness in the chest.

Fear affects us physically, emotionally, mentally, spiritually, and socially. Fear causes a hesitancy in relationships because self-protective walls are built. These are invisible walls, but very real. Fear prohibits one from getting close to others. A fearful person has difficulty being vulnerable. The feeling is that if one allows herself to be vulnerable and reveal who she really is, then she may be rejected. This is just too scary.

Whole Again

By B. Kay Coulter

Whole again—Jesus make me whole again.
Create in me a clean heart,
Giving me a fresh start.
Whole again—Jesus make me whole again.
For it's in You I can be new.
Deep in my soul I can be whole again.
I gave my life to Jesus so very long ago.
Just like a newborn baby I needed to grow.
And grow I did through trials and pain.
But since I came to Jesus I've never been the same.
With Jesus I've known joy.
I've known abundant life.
I've known His love and mercy in the midst of strife.
Tested in temptation, battered by sin,
I can come to Jesus, for He makes me whole again.
Whole again—Jesus, make me whole again.
Create in me a clean heart,
Giving me a fresh start.
Whole again—Jesus, make me whole again.
For it's in You I can be new.
Deep in my soul I can be whole again.

CHAPTER SIX

Journey From Fear to Faith

How does one get out of this trap of fear and this endless cycle of fear and guilt? God has provided a way through His Son Jesus. He has communicated to us a message of hope. One can see God's provision throughout the Bible as angels arrived upon the human scene with messages of hope. Time and time again, they encouraged the fearful to "fear not." The phrase "fear not" is found 365 times in the Bible—one for each day of the year.

There are antidotes to the poison of fear. I would like to explore some of them in this chapter. First of all, we must *believe* God is who He says He is, as David expressed *his* belief in Psalm 55:23b: "But as for me, I trust in you." Only when we believe who God is can we begin to understand who we are. When we understand that we are created by a loving God, we have the framework within which God can help us understand our worth.

In Luke 12:7, our worth is affirmed: "Don't be afraid; you are worth more than many sparrows." Second Timothy 1:7 (KJV) promises: "For God hath not given us a spirit of fear, but a spirit of power, of love and of a sound mind." There is also the promise in 1 John 4:18: "There is no fear in love. Perfect love casts out fear."

What is perfect love? Or better yet, who is the source of perfect love? First John 4:7a says, "Dear friends, let us love one another, for love comes from God." God is the source of love, for He *is* love. Love originates with Him. If you are seeking perfect love from any other source, you will be sorely disappointed. It is only the perfect love of God that enables us to overcome our fears.

For centuries millions of people have drawn comfort from the famous twenty-third Psalm. This beautiful psalm written by David illustrates well the love of God. Perhaps you are very familiar with Psalm twenty-three, but you need to take a fresh look to see how the God of love is depicted here.

> The LORD is my shepherd, I shall not
> be in want.
> He makes me lie down in green
> pastures,
> he leads me beside quiet waters,
> he restores my soul.
> He guides me in paths of
> righteousness
> for his name's sake.
> Even though I walk
> through the valley of the shadow of
> death,
> I will fear no evil,
> for you are with me;
> your rod and your staff,
> they comfort me.
>
> You prepare a table before me
> in the presence of my enemies.
> You anoint my head with oil;
> my cup overflows.
> Surely goodness and love will follow
> me

all the days of my life,
and I will dwell in the house of the
LORD forever.

Do you see the great love of the Father in this passage? I see God as provider, nurturer, leader, restorer, comforter. I see the gentle, loving nature of God in the way He cares for His "sheep" (His people). I see the generosity of God as He gives until "my cup overflows." I see His affirmation of my worth as He "prepare[s] a table before me in the presence of my enemies." I see the security that God provides in the promise that "I will dwell in the house of the LORD forever." All these things—provision, nurturing, guidance, restoration, comfort, generosity, affirmation, and security—flow out of His love for me. It is because I know God loves me that I "fear no evil." David knew of the love of God, and the Psalms reveal how he appealed to it many times when He was in need:

Remember, O LORD, your great mercy
and love,
for they are from of old. (25:6)

Your love, O LORD, reaches to the
heavens,
your faithfulness to the skies....
How priceless is your unfailing
love. (36:5 and 7)
Because your love is better than life,
my lips will glorify you. (63:3)
When I said, "My foot is slipping,"
your love, O LORD, supported me. (94:18)

I will sing of your love and justice;
to you, O LORD, I will sing praise. (101:1)

For as high as the heavens are above
the earth,
so great is his love for those who
fear him. (103:11)

Give thanks to the LORD, for he is
good;
his love endures forever. (118:1)

Such is the nature of our Father's perfect love. In return, we need to express our love to Him. The Psalmist David had a great love relationship with the Creator of perfect love, as is evidenced in Psalm 18:1—"I love you, O LORD, my strength."

LOVE

The first antidote that is recommended, therefore, for the poison of fear is love—unconditional love. God's love to us is expressed in many ways, not the least of which is through the Psalms, a book filled with comfort and encouragement. He loves us so much that He wants us to know how to overcome fear. In the Psalms there is both admonition to overcome fear and comfort for those who are afraid.

First of all, we have the admonition from God—do not fret or worry. We know that fretting and worrying rise out of fearfulness and can have no good outcome. Worry in itself can keep us in bondage to fear. God wants us to turn loose of our fear and recognize that He can be trusted. This can be done when we change our focus from ourselves and our problems to a focus on God.

PRAISE

Praise is a very effective way to focus on God—on who He is. No book of the Bible has as much to say about the practice of praise as does the Psalms. An example is Psalm 150:

Praise ye the LORD.

Praise God in His sanctuary;
praise Him in the firmament of His power.
praise Him for His mighty acts:
praise Him according to His excellent greatness.

Praise Him with the sound of the trumpet:
praise Him with the psaltery and harp,
praise Him with the timbrel and dance:
praise Him with stringed instruments and organs.
praise Him upon the loud cymbals:
praise Him upon the high sounding cymbals.
Let every thing that hath breath praise the LORD.

Praise ye the LORD. (KJV)

Praise focuses our attention on God as we pray, as we sing, and as we meditate. God has promised that He "inhabit(s) the praises of His people" (Psalm 22:3b KJV). When we are filled with praise, directing our thoughts toward God, it is impossible to be filled with fear and dread.

When we are praising God, it means that we have humble and grateful hearts: "I am under vows to you, O God; I will present my thank offerings to You" (Psalm 56:12). We can overcome our enemy, the devil, by proclaiming our praise. I have heard it said that praise (as thankfulness) is to God what whining, complaining, and criticizing is to Satan. Psalm 56:3-4 reaffirms that praise is a good antidote to the poison of fear:

> When I am afraid,
> I will trust in You.
> In God, whose word I praise,
> in God I trust; I will not be afraid.
> What can mortal man do to me?

There is much healing power in praise. Praise is a wonderful antidote for fear because it lifts us to the level of God's *perspective*, reminds us of God's *power*, reviews God's *promises*, and fills our hearts with a *praise* attitude which overcomes our fear.

I have experienced this truth for myself on many occasions. One such occasion was when I was preparing to sing in my church at Christmas time. I found myself slipping back into the bondage of anxiety. I had been feeling depressed for several weeks and was not feeling positively about singing in my church on Christmas Eve. As a matter of fact, I had little motivation to sing at all! However, God was faithful to keep me from slipping too far. As the day drew near for my performance I knew I would need to practice in order to be well prepared, so I just set my mind to the task. My song of choice was "O Magnify the LORD." As I began to practice this wonderful praise song, a transformation began to take shape in me—particularly when I started quoting aloud the words of the Magnificat that I paired with the song. (Mary's words of praise at the announcement brought to her by Gabriel are the Magnificat. Luke 1:46-55) My spirit of anxiety lifted; I was able to genuinely praise God; and I began experiencing a turning point in my deliverance from depression.

From my own personal experience I have found the most effective way to set my voice to singing God's praises is to play music that lifts my soul heavenward. I advise this activity as a wonderful way to overcome fear. Fill your house, your car, and most of all, your heart with Christian music.

Filling your heart with His music will fill your mind with reminders of His faithfulness.

READ AND REMEMBER

With all the distractions and trials of this life, we often need to be reminded of God's faithfulness. Reviewing God's promises means remembering what God has done for us in the past.

> Praise our God, O peoples,
> let the sound of His praise be heard;
> he has preserved our lives
> and kept our feet from slipping. (Psalm 66:8-9)

Our faith is built up one day at a time, so it is helpful if we look back over the years of our lives and identify those times when God has strengthened us or provided for us in some way. Psalm 84:5 says, "Blessed are those whose strength is in you, who have set their hearts on pilgrimage..." Life indeed is a pilgrimage. When I confront obstacles in my path, it is good to remember that God has enabled me in the past to overcome obstacles. Remembering and reflecting on these times strengthens my mind and soul. The following psalm speaks of a weak, delicate creature of which God takes great care. This creature is a sparrow. I identify with the sparrow, and I am encouraged by this passage:

> Even the sparrow has found a home,
> and the swallow a nest for herself,
> where she may have her young—
> a place near your altar,
> O LORD Almighty, my King and
> my God.
> Blessed are those who dwell in your
> house,
> they are ever praising you. (Psalm 84:3-4)

It is easy for me to identify with this particular sparrow, for, like the sparrow, I felt like a delicate creature who needed a shelter—a haven where I could be nurtured. As a child I needed a haven for the nurturing of my soul. Though my parents did provide for my physical needs, I had to look elsewhere to have my emotional needs met. God provided for me by drawing me "near [*his*] altar." Even as a very young child I had a real sense of God's presence and loved to be in His church. *He* was my haven. I used to think I had an invisible friend whom I called Lulu. I could tell this friend anything and be myself without being afraid. This friend was a comfort to me when I was troubled. As an adult I now see that this friend was Jesus, who related to me on the level of my child-like understanding. Since I couldn't rely on my parents to meet my deepest needs, I needed someone else in whom I could place my trust. What I thought was an imagined presence, I now understand was actually a manifestation of God's presence, providing my needed haven. My response to His presence has always been to praise Him through singing. Like the protected sparrow that is filled with song, so I have been filled with song. Praise has been a powerful means to bring me to a place of wholeness. I believe this is what is meant by God's "inhabiting" our praise.

EXERCISE THE WILL

The aforementioned verses, Psalm 56:3-4, give us another clue to overcoming fear. Notice the phrases "I *will* trust" and "I *will not* be afraid." If we want deliverance from bondage, we must exercise our wills—make a choice! This is not to say that our deliverance merely depends on our ability to exercise "mind over matter," to practice "positive thinking," or to depend upon our own willpower. However, exercising the will (making the decision) not to be afraid and to trust God is an essential element in the process of healing. Verse seven of

Psalms 37 gives us a command: "Be still…do not fret." This is not a suggestion or a hint. God is challenging us to make the decision to "not fret." This injunction from Scripture reminds me of when I had small children. With children, it is essential that the parent establish his/her authority very early in the child's life. I can remember many times when I had to say to my child, "Be still!" Usually when I demanded this action, I was wanting my child's attention. I expected my child to obey me, and I knew that if he did he would be blessed. He did have a choice. He could have chosen to disobey me, and sometimes disobedience was his choice. When he obeyed me, however, he was ready to give me his attention. When I had his full attention, then I could further instruct him in ways that would benefit him. I believe that our Father God is like this with us. He gives the command to "Be still!" so He can have our full attention. When we give up our willfulness and give attention to God's instructions, we are blessed. At the very least, our relationship with our Father is developed to a higher level. It is then we are open to receive the blessings God has for us, and we will be stronger to face our fears. Let us say with the Psalmist,

> When I am afraid,
> I will trust in You.
> In God, whose word I praise,
> in God I trust; I will not be afraid.
>
> What can mortal man do to me?" (Psalm 56:3-4)

Expressing our praise and exercising our wills result in our learning to trust in God. As we trust God, we are then free to choose His paths for our journey.

CALL UPON GOD

If we are to receive God's help to overcome our fears, we

must first call upon Him. It seems this act would be obvious and we would naturally think of it in times of trouble. However, it is amazing to me how many people do not even think about calling upon God for help. The Psalms give us many examples of David's calling upon God in his times of trouble. Let these serve as reminders to us:

> Answer me when I call to you,
> O my righteous God.
> Give me relief from my distress;
> be merciful to me and hear my
> prayer. (4:1)
>
> Give ear to my words, O LORD,
> consider my sighing.
> Listen to my cry for help,
> my King and my God,
> for to you I pray. (5:1-2)
>
> Help, LORD, for the godly are no
> more.... (12:1)
>
> Keep me safe, O God,
> for in you I take refuge. (16:1)
>
> Hear, O LORD, my righteous plea;
> listen to my cry.
> Give ear to my prayer.... (17:1)
>
> To you I call, O LORD my Rock;
> do not turn a deaf ear to me. (28:1a)
>
> Have mercy on me, O God,
> according to your unfailing love.... (51:1)
>
> My soul yearns, even faints,
> for the courts of the LORD;

> my heart and my flesh cry out
> for the living God. (84:2)
>
> Search me, O God, and know my
> heart.... (139:23)
>
> Give thanks to the LORD, call on his
> name.... (105:1)
>
> The LORD is near to all who call on
> him,
> to all who call on Him in truth. (145:18)

Other Scripture passages also encourage us to call upon God:

> Seek the LORD while he may be
> found;
> call on him while he is near. (Isaiah 55:6)
>
> Call to me and I will answer you and tell you great and unsearchable things you do not know.
> (Jeremiah 33:3)
>
> Everyone who calls upon the name of the LORD will be saved. (Romans 10:12)

This matter of calling upon the LORD should be done in sincerity and in truth (Psalm 145:18). Unfortunately, in our day, many do use the name of God in times of distress but their cries of "O my God" do not come from a genuine request for God's help. God desires that we call out to Him because He knows He can answer our prayers. But more than this He is seeking a loving relationship with us. Let us not be flippant with our words, taking God's name in vain (Exodus 20:7), but rather let us be sincere of heart as we respond to His love.

NAME YOUR ENEMIES

In calling upon God to help, we should be specific when we express our needs. In his praying, David was very specific about his needs, and he often identified his enemies. Not only did David have obvious enemies in the form of people who were against him, but there were physical "enemies" (ill health) and psychological "enemies" (depression, etc.) as well. I relate to David in this area of psychological enemies. When I have been in need, such as in times of depression, the Psalms have brought me great comfort.

In identifying my "enemies" my mind is brought into sharp focus. Also, when I am specific about what is troubling me and present these specifics to the LORD, I am better aware of His answers when they come. On one occasion as I meditated on Psalm 56:9, God helped me to identify some of the enemies I had encountered in my life. This verse reads, "Then my enemies will turn back when I call for help. By this I will know that God is for me." The enemies that came to mind were:

- Those who abuse me
- Memories of abuse.
- Fear and shame.
- Depression.
- Inability to act.

Perhaps for you there are other enemies, but whatever they are, it is necessary to identify them and call upon God for help in defeating them. We have His promise that "enemies will turn back." I believe God is anxious to prove to us that He is on our side. He desires to deliver us from our enemy, even if the enemy is within us. Sometimes feelings can be enemies. As we give in to certain feelings, we often become overwhelmed and cannot see a way out of our difficulties. To avoid becoming a lifelong "victim," it is necessary to identify the feelings, which in this case are our responses to victimization. We must choose to allow God to take control rather than allowing the feelings to control us.

DO GOOD

When we free ourselves from feelings that overwhelm us, we become free to focus on others' needs. Psalm 37:3 says, "Trust in the LORD and do good." Can you see how we can walk without fear and with a new confidence when we have learned to trust God? We become free to focus on others, because we know our needs are provided for by a loving God. When we give up our fear and we trust God, He frees us to "do good" to others. However, this is a choice we must make—choosing to do good despite the evil that's been done to us. The act of trusting God and doing good changes our focus. As we lift our eyes heavenward, praising God from sincere hearts, our vision becomes clear. With this new vision, we are better able to relate to others and better able to put their needs ahead of ours.

As a singer, I had many feelings of insecurity to overcome in my journey from fear to faith. A close friend of mine who has witnessed my journey told me she began to see the difference in my singing as I began to feel secure in who I am—"fearfully and wonderfully made" (Psalm 139:14). With this secure foundation, I found that I was much less self-conscious. Over time, as I have grown in my newly found confidence, I have been able to sing boldly and freely, with my focus on worshipping God and ministering to others. I no longer worry so much about making mistakes (although I still believe in preparing well). When I stand before an audience, I do not have to be a "star" giving a perfect performance. I realize that this occasion is not about me but about God's "doing good" through me. When I lose myself, others are free to focus their attention on the song and its message. What freedom!

You, of course, do not have to be a public performer to "do good" to others. There are many ways in which we can minister to others and many times in which we will not even draw attention to ourselves. We will explore in a later chapter more about ministry.

COMMIT

We must trust God for guidance as we seek to be healed of past abuse. Psalm 37:5 says, "Commit your way to the LORD." Committing to something or someone means overcoming fears and doubts and being willing to take risks. When we do this, we are giving God priority in our lives and can claim the promise of Psalm 37:4: "Delight yourself in the LORD, and He will give you the desires of your heart."

When we give God priority in our lives, there is room for growth and vision in our hearts. With this growth and vision we can experience His love in a more real way. Only when we commit ourselves to God can we have genuine hope of healing. Though there be much darkness within me (because of my own sinfulness and the sins against me), God has said: "He will make your [my] righteousness shine like the dawn" (Psalm 37:6).

How can this be? What does it mean, anyway, to be righteous? The word "righteousness" as it is used in the Old Testament means "to be straight," or, "to conform to one's divinely created human nature." It also means "to fulfill one's proper role in life." I admit that this is not a word that is used much in our society. Righteousness means to be in right standing with God. It might be equated with morality or virtue, but it has a deeper meaning than either of these words. Morality and virtue are qualities that can be attained by human efforts. Righteousness is something that one cannot attain on his own. It is only through believing in Jesus Christ and taking on His righteousness that one can claim any promise given to the righteous, such as is in 1 Peter 3:1: "For Christ died for sins once for all, the righteous for the unrighteous, to bring you to God.". The availability of Christ's righteousness to us is good news since we can't be righteous on our own. The New Testament was written so we could know this good news, as is illustrated in Acts 16:31(AMP): "Believe in *and* on the Lord Jesus *Christ*—that is, give yourself up to Him, take yourself out of your own keeping and entrust yourself into his keeping, and you will be saved...."

I cannot depend on my own righteousness to save me, for even the best of us is flawed by sin. When we try to depend on our own righteousness, it is as if we put clean garments (of our own choosing) on a filthy body. We may fool some people and we may even fool ourselves, but God knows the truth. We cannot cover up our sinfulness. I am reminded of this clean-garment analogy as I think of my own wardrobe. I have a washable silk blouse that seems to attract stains. After many unfruitful attempts at cleaning it myself, I finally took it to a professional dry cleaner, in hopes that he would be able to eliminate the stains. The trouble is, the very first time I wear it again I manage to drip something on it, usually in front where it can be clearly seen. This is very frustrating, and I wonder if it is worth wearing at all!

Is this not like our feeble attempts to clean ourselves up by trying to reform? We may feel clean for a while because we "act righteously," but before long we get our self-righteous garment soiled and stained by our sinful behavior. It is essential, therefore, that we allow God to cleanse us through the righteousness of Jesus. It is then that we can "walk before God in the light of life" (Psalm 56:13).

Verse six of Psalm 37 reads: "He will make your righteousness shine like the dawn, the justice of your cause like the noonday sun." As we bring our cause to God (our need for healing), we can know that God will judge our abusers and will defend us. Many scriptures speak of God's taking on the cause of the oppressed. Some from the Psalms are:

> Because of the oppression of the
> weak
> and the groaning of the needy,
> I will now arise," says the LORD.
> "I will protect them from those who
> malign them." (Psalm 12:5)

> He only is my rock and my salvation;
> he is my fortress; I will not be
> shaken. (Psalm 62:6)

> The LORD is a refuge for the
> oppressed,
> a stronghold in times of trouble. (Psalm 9:9)

HOPE

God, through His promises, gives us hope—hope that we can be vindicated in the wrongs that have been done to us, and hope that we can be freed from our bondage to fear.

> Trust in the LORD and do good;
> dwell in the land and enjoy safe
> pasture. (Psalm 37:3)

> But the meek will inherit the land
> and enjoy great peace. (37:11)

Contrary to general opinion, the "meek" are not those who are weakened by fear. The meek are those who have a proper and realistic view of their place in God's Kingdom. Many times people associate the word "meek" with "weak." The words are not synonymous! To get an idea of the meaning of "meek," imagine a powerful stallion. The stallion may be beautiful to look at and strong enough to roam free, but he is of no use to man until he allows himself to be broken and trained. Then a bit can be put in his mouth, which will cause him to be responsive to every pull of the reins attached to it. As the stallion submits to his master, he becomes a tool in the master's hands to be used for good. His power and strength is no less than before he was trained. However, now his power is available to allow the master to accomplish great things. Meekness, then, is power under control. A note on Matthew 5:5 in the *NIV Study Bible* says meekness refers "not so much to an attitude toward man as to a disposition before God, namely, humility." Victims are afraid of weakness because they have been overpowered by someone in the past. But if a victim puts himself in the hands of God in meekness and humility, he then can rest in the Almighty One.

Another one of the fears a victim has is that her abuser will not be punished, but rather get away with his abuse. One thing we need to entrust to the Lord is the punishment of the abuser. We can trust God to carry out justice, for He is a just God. He is also the only One who can rightly assess the need for punishment and the extent of the punishment. He sees all the consequences of a person's actions and knows how many people will be affected.

1 Corinthians 4:5 tells us that, "He will bring to light what is hidden in darkness and will expose the motives of men's hearts." God in His wisdom has promised:

> ...the wicked will be no more. (Psalm 37:10)

> The wicked plot against the righteous
> and gnash their teeth at them;
> for he knows their day is coming. (37:12-13)

> The wicked draw the sword...
> But their swords will pierce their own
> hearts,
> and their bows will be broken. (37:14-15)

> The wicked will perish. (37:20)
>
> ...those he curses will be cut off. (37:22)
>
> ...but the offspring of the wicked will be cut off. (37:29)

Although to our finite minds it may appear that the wicked triumph, we know for certain that God will punish them. They will suffer in many ways for their sins, and the power of their abuse will be broken. The wicked have no assurance for their future as do the righteous, and they have no promise of God's protection.

The unrepentant person has no right to expect God to bless him, but the person who seeks to please God can expect His blessings. God reassures the fearful through the promises in His Word. There are many such promises throughout the Bible, including our area of concentration—the Psalms. We will examine these promises in the next chapter.

CHAPTER SEVEN

A Sure Foundation

One promise that has captured my attention is Psalm 37:31, which reads, "The law of God is in his heart, his feet do not slip." First of all, we must ask who receives this promise of "not slipping." It is given to the one who knows "the law of God in his heart." Putting God's laws in our hearts involves more than having an intellectual understanding of the words. This speaks to me of the importance of reading, studying, meditating on, and memorizing God's Word. When we move beyond just knowledge of the truth to the application of it in our lives, we can know we really do have God's laws in our hearts. As God's laws are ever before me, the path I am to follow will be clear. I do not have to remain on the miry, slippery path that my parents set before me. If I choose to be bitter and refuse God's healing, however, I will remain on the slippery path, making my steps falter all along my journey through life. "Slipping" suggests an unsure footing or a shaky foundation and will be manifested in the following ways:

- Insecurity
- Lack of balance (emotional instability)

- Negative thinking
- Verbal abuse
- Weaknesses of temperament
- Feelings of inferiority
- Anger
- Lack of trust
- Promiscuity
- Faithlessness
- Hampered relationship to God
- Spiritual blindness and deafness

SECURITY

This list looks very much like the symptoms of a victim of abuse, does it not? If these symptoms, or elements of slipping, are still evident years after the abuse took place, there is a need for the victim to turn to the One who can give him a sure foundation. God desires that we build our lives on the sure foundation He provides, because He knows what is best for us. He promises us that we can walk steadily through life if we place our trust in Him:

> His feet do not slip. (Psalm 37:31)

> He makes my feet like the feet of a
> deer;
> he enables me to stand on the heights. (18:33)

> Your word is a lamp to my feet
> and a light for my path. (119:105)

> He lifted me out of the slimy pit,
> out of the mud and mire;
> he set my feet on a rock
> and gave me a firm place to stand. (40:2)

The imagery here is wonderful! Who among us does not

need a firm foundation for life? Who among us does not desire to have a clearly marked path to follow on our journey through life? Can you see how the choices we make bring about serious consequences in our lives? We can choose the muddy, slimy, slippery path of uncertainty by choosing *not* to trust in God. Or, we can choose to trust in Him and to have stability as we journey down *His* paths.

We know that fear and faith cannot occupy the same space, so we must come to the point of allowing God to replace our fear with faith. God desires to bring us to a place of hope and peace. Hope and peace provide a firm foundation, from which we can begin our journey of healing.

> The fruit of righteousness will be
> peace;
> the effect of righteousness will be
> quietness and confidence forever. (Isaiah 32:17)

TRUST

Although God can bring us along the way to hope and peace, we are required to reach up and take His hand. This requires that we embark on a journey—I call it the journey of healing—that takes us from fear to faith. This is not an easy task, of course, for there are many roadblocks along the way. Yet, there are signposts as well—signs from God's Word, the testimonies of others, and answers to prayer. Along this path there will also be forks in the road. There are choices to be made at these junctures. Our ultimate healing depends on these choices. How is one able to replace fear with trust? I believe that it begins with an act of the will—deciding to trust. This is not blind faith but a faith based on fact. The facts of God's faithfulness are clearly demonstrated in the lives of people in the Bible and also in the lives of our contemporaries. These facts provide the signposts on the road to healing. We need only look to the past to see God at work. The testimonies of millions over the centuries of time shout out His faithfulness. Years ago, in a time of fearfulness and uncertainty, I was reminded of the truth of God's faithfulness when I read Jeremiah 6:16:

> Thus said the LORD, "Stand ye in the ways, and see, and ask for the old paths, where is the good way, and walk therein, and ye shall find rest for you souls.' (KJV)

> For everything that was written in the past was written to teach us, so that through endurance and the encouragement of the Scriptures we might have hope. (Romans 15:4)

I could see that many had traveled the "old ways" before me. By studying how they made the journey, my faith could be rebuilt. As I saw how He had worked before, my eyes were opened to His working in the present, and I was assured that He would continue to do so in the future.

It is true that we should take a look backward in order to know what has gone before, but we must also look ahead to know our destination. At the end of the road is a place of *peace* and *freedom*, and we begin the journey by letting go of our fears and turning them over to God. He is, after all, the only completely trustworthy One to whom we can give ourselves. It bears repeating: God created us and loves us and desires what is best for us. We must believe this if we are to know true freedom from bondage. In order to know who we really *are*, we must go to The One who caused us to *be* in the first place. In order to love ourselves and others, we must first accept God's gift of love to us—Jesus Christ. In order to know the way in which to go, we must look to the omniscient One who knows the beginning and the end. We need to change our view of ourselves from an inadequate self-centered view to a fully adequate Christ-centered view.

SELF-WORTH

Typically, victims have a view of ourselves that does not reveal our true value. By committing our lives to Christ, we can know our true value—a value that is not based on performance or the opinions of others. I remember that I came to really understand my value as I internalized the truth of Psalm 139:13-16:

> For you created my inmost being;
> you knit me together in my
> mother's womb.
>
> I praise you because I am fearfully and
> wonderfully made;
> your works are wonderful,
> I know that full well.
>
> My frame was not hidden from you
> when I was made in the secret
> place.
>
> When I was woven together in the
> depths of the earth,
> your eyes saw my unformed body.
>
> All the days ordained for me
> were written in your book
> before one of them came to be.

Imagine that! The great and awesome God of the universe attends to even the intricate details of my creation and my earthly journey. It is as though God has invested Himself in me and receives a dividend on that investment from my success in living. He has a very personal interest in me and has gone to great lengths to reveal Himself and His character, as well as to give instructions for living a victorious life. Do I not then owe it to Him to learn those instructions? Dear Reader, are you beginning to get a picture of why it is that we can trust God? As we come to trust Him, we can begin to love Him, and we know that "perfect love casts out fear" (I John 4:18). If we want to be overcomers, living by faith, we must receive His love.

When we feel loved, we feel secure. The typical victim does not feel safe and secure, is suspicious of everyone, and is lacking in trust. Let me encourage you to give up the chains of insecurity and fear. When our hands are released from the shackles of our insecurity, we can then reach up and place our hands in God's hand. In my mind's eye, I can see God's hand—the *miracle-working* hand that created the universe, the *mighty* hand that defeated His enemies, the *gentle* hand that comforted His people, and the *firm* hand that led His people out of bondage. His is the hand that upholds the righteous. God has worked in the past and is still at work today to give His children security. This is security, indeed!

BELONGING

Another fear of victims is that we are "invisible." We wonder if anyone really knows us or cares about our feelings. God has said He cares—He knows the days of the blameless. We are not invisible to Him. Remember Psalm 139:16, which states that all my days "were written in your book...." God knows us best because He created us, and He cares what happens to us.

When we allow fear to control us we are blind to God's promises, and we are overtaken with an emotional poison. If we do not deal with this poison of fear, we will continue the abusive patterns that were passed on to us by our parents. The normal pattern of abuse is cyclical, being passed from one generation to the next. The generational pattern can be broken, however, by the choices we make. When a person decides to follow God's path of righteousness (way of right living), he is released from bondage and can find true healing. For those who break the cycle of abuse and live uprightly, they will pass on to their children a godly inheritance which "will endure forever" (Psalm 37:18b).

Our sense of security, then, comes from God as we place our trust in Him and take on His righteousness. It is He who makes us secure. Just as He promised to be security for His people Israel, He promises security to us, His children born of faith.

> But now, this is what the LORD says—
> he Who created you, O Jacob,
> he who formed you, O Israel:
> "Fear not, for I have redeemed you;
> I have summoned you by name;
> you are mine.
>
> When you pass through the waters,
> I will be with you;
> and when you pass through the rivers,
> they will not sweep over you.
> When you walk through the fire,
> you will not be burned;
> the flames will not set you ablaze." (Isaiah 43:1-2)

With this sense of security you can dare to live life to the fullest. People will disappoint you and abuse you, but your security is not in what others think of you, but rather in Christ Jesus, the Perfect One who never disappoints. It is only when your security is well placed in God that you can be free to take risks, giving of yourself for the sake of others. Psalm 37:21 says, "The wicked borrow and do not repay, but the righteous give generously." The abuser is a taker only, desperately trying to acquire things or people to fill his emptiness. The righteous is secure and can freely give because his needs are met by the Lord. With this sense of security that comes from the Lord, there comes a settledness within, eliminating the need for grasping and striving.

HOPE

Not only do we have security for our present living but we also have a hope for the future—the hope of overcoming, as is expressed in Psalm 37:23-24:

> If the LORD delights in a man's way,
> he makes his steps firm;
> though he stumble, he will not fall,
> for the LORD upholds him with his
> hand.

Part of the insecurity evident in a victim comes from a sense of having been abandoned, for a sense of abandonment is common among victims. If a child is neglected by parents (physically or emotionally), he feels abandoned. If a child is abused, he feels abandoned by the one who should have nurtured him. If a child does not have a sense of worth and value, he even feels abandoned by God. There is good news, however, for those of us who have felt abandoned by our earthly loved ones. God promises never to abandon us, as the Psalmist acknowledges in 37:25-26, saying he'd "never seen the righteous forsaken." Fearful people tend to cling to a faulty foundation—that of a low self-worth.

I can identify with the person who has responded to abuse and neglect with fear. What are we afraid of? We are afraid of being hurt, of what others will say, of not measuring up to what we perceive as the standards others set for us. It is as if we clutch within our grasp our very souls. We are afraid to give up these perceptions of ourselves because we believe the lies which others have communicated to us through their verbal and physical abuse. Our very identities are tied up in these perceptions. We think, "It might not be much, but it's all I have." However, we do not have to be characterized by fear. There is a way out of fear.

FAITH

The way out of fear is to get on the pathway of faith. It is only when we exercise faith that we can be free—free to walk steadily through life. The Bible speaks of this pathway as the "path of righteousness" (right standing with God). Come along with me on this journey from fear to faith as we walk the "path of righteousness."

CHAPTER EIGHT

The Paths of Righteousness

If we sincerely want to be freed from the bondage of past hurts, we must change our perceptions—about God and about ourselves. Once we come to believe God and to believe in ourselves, we then can commit ourselves to Him, trusting that He will lead us to healing. We don't just cast out our fears but rather cast all our cares upon God ("Cast all your anxiety on him because he cares for you." 1 Peter 5:7). Though victims try many paths in order to find peace (the absence of fear), all routes lead to a dead-end if they do not follow God's path. God's path is the path of righteousness. At the end of the path is perfect peace and freedom. I have listed here a few other things that we can expect to find on this path:

- Cleansing forgiveness
- Peace of mind
- Joy
- Freedom from bitterness
- The ability to give and receive love
- Spiritual riches
- A good name
- Purity before God

- Guidance for daily living
- Communion with God
- Hope for this life
- Eternal security

Is there anyone among us who does not desire these things? Many times it is hard for the victim to believe that he deserves all this or can even have all this, but it is possible. God has promised us, and He does not go back on His promises. Psalm 37:11 says, "But the meek will inherit the land and enjoy great peace." And Psalm 37:16 says, "Better the little the righteous have than the wealth of many wicked." Other Psalms that speak about these promises to the righteous are:

> ...the LORD upholds the righteous. (37:17)
>
> The days of the blameless are known to
> the LORD. (37:18)
>
> In times of disaster they will not wither;
> in days of famine, they will enjoy
> plenty. (37:19)
>
> ...those the LORD blesses will inherit the
> land.... (37:22)
>
> Wait for the LORD
> and keep His way...
> he will exalt you to inherit the land.... (37:34)
>
> Consider the blameless, observe the
> upright;
> there is a future for the man of
> peace. (37:37)

These promises were given to David at a time after He had been victimized. He had been targeted for death by King Saul on many occasions, as the king saw him as a threat to the throne. He had suffered from attacks of malicious slander from those he called friends (Psalm 35:19-20). He was betrayed by his own son Absalom (2 Samuel 15-17). He had suffered the pangs of a parent whose children had gone astray (2 Samuel 13). At times David responded to that victimization with fear. Psalm 56:1-6 reveals his fearful heart:

> Be merciful to me, O God, for men
> hotly pursue me;
> all day long they press their attack.
>
> My slanderers pursue me all day long;
> many are attacking me in their
> pride.
> When I am afraid,
> I will trust in you.
>
> In God, whose word I praise,
> In God I trust; I will not be afraid.
> What can mortal man do to me?
>
> All day long they twist my words;
> they are always plotting to harm me.
>
> They conspire, they lurk,
> they watch my steps,
> eager to take my life.

These verses remind me of what it is like to be a victim who is still in bondage to her past. I am one who for years carried the baggage of past hurts. Before I came to God for healing, fear governed me in several ways. There was the feeling that I was ever being pursued and attacked. The fear that I experienced was manifested in different ways. Many times as I walked along the street, I kept looking around to see if I were being followed. I felt the need to be apologetic about most of my actions as though someone were standing over me, judging me. It was the inner pain that I carried that caused me to feel under attack. In this kind of fear, the victim feels that more abuse will come—even expects it to come. It was so freeing when I began to realize that I did not have to go through life feeling apologetic for my existence. God gave me a new confidence to be what He desired me to be and an assurance that I did not have to worry about what others might think or do. It was as if He encircled me with an invisible shield that warded off both real and imagined attacks upon my self-worth.

In my journey from fear to faith, I first had to realize my innate worth. Psalm 139 taught me my true worth as one of God's creations. The New Testament showed me in a greater way my worth to God as I came to place my faith in Christ. Not only am I created by God but I am also redeemed by Him. He loved me enough to save me from my sinful state and to give me a new life—a life that can be lived victoriously through the power of Jesus Christ.

2 Corinthians 5:17 illustrates this truth: "Therefore, if anyone is in Christ, he is a new creation; the old has gone, the new has come!" (NIV) Further steps on my journey to healing included:

- Revisiting my past, taking Jesus with me in my mind.
- Recognizing the bondage of fear that was still present in my life.
- Seeking godly help through a Christian counselor.
- Acknowledging the hurts and grieving over them.
- Asking God to heal the hurts.
- Acknowledging my own sin (bad choices); repenting;

receiving God's forgiveness.
- Forgiving those who had hurt me.
- Practicing a newfound freedom by trusting God.

The promises in the Bible are to the upright, or righteous (those in good standing with God). How does one become righteous? The Bible teaches that "all have sinned and come short of the glory of God" (Romans 3:23). None of us can measure up to God's standard of righteousness, but God does not give us an impossible command. Instead, He offers the Way to righteousness—Jesus Christ. When we place our faith in Jesus, believing that He died to save us from our sins, then we take on *His* righteousness. Clothed in Jesus' righteousness we can claim God's promises to the righteous.

> That if you confess with your mouth, "Jesus is Lord," and believe in your heart that God raised him from the dead, you will be saved. For it is with your heart that you believe and are justified, and it is with your mouth that you confess and are saved. (Romans 10:9-10)

Once we know that our salvation is secured through Christ, we have hope that we can overcome our fears. Remember the road signs along the journey from fear to faith (see chapter six):

- Love
- Praise
- Remember
- Exercise the will
- Trust
- Call upon God
- Name your enemies
- Do good
- Commit

- Hope
- Walk steadily

In following God's path to healing, I have indeed found freedom for living a victorious life, and so can you. I believe that every victim can find this same freedom by choosing to follow God's path. The Gospel is Good News to all of us. We do not have to remain in bondage to fear. We can be free—free to be all God created us to be!

CHAPTER NINE

Poison: Anger

Another response to abuse is anger. The person who responds in anger develops an angry disposition that will control him throughout his life if it is not acknowledged and dealt with. Anger is the emotion that motivates and drives him. He is looking for justice and vengeance because of what has been done to him, and he feels compelled to action in order to carry out the vengeance himself. The anger is evident in the way he looks, acts, and sounds.

A person with an angry disposition is intense, with jaw set, eyes steely, posture rigid. He may also tend to clinch his fists, slam doors, etc. We are all familiar with this type who has a bad day, with conflict at work, heavy traffic, etc., comes in the door and kicks the family pet. He's mad at the world in general, and it doesn't take much to set him off on a tirade. His blood pressure is frequently high, and he probably tends to both get ulcers and give them to others because of his behavior. This way of life can be deadly to his health, of course. Dr. Ichiro Kawachi, assistant professor of medicine at Harvard University, surveyed a group of 1,305 Veterans Administration patients. This survey was reported on in November, 1996. Dr. Kawachi states:

> Such extreme anger increased risk of coronary heart disease two to three times above their relaxed counterparts. And the angrier they are, the higher their risk. We're talking about extreme anger here. From the kinds of questions we asked the subjects, some felt like exploding, others were constantly irritable and grouchy—still others would hurt furniture and even other people. This is not the common, garden-variety irritation that we might feel. Such anger triggers the body's "fight or flight" mechanism that releases stress hormones into the bloodstream and slows the progress of platelets, which form clots that can begin a heart attack. Two 1994 studies showed that men with high levels of anxiety were at four to six times the risk of fatal heart disease than men who had no symptoms.[18]

There have been many studies showing the effects of anger upon the health of the individual. Suffice it to say that carrying long-term angry feelings is not healthy.

What does an angry person sound like? Her words will be terse, blunt, and harsh, and she will be an expert at cut-downs. Many times this person will speak through clinched teeth. She also will tend to slam doors, pound her fist on the table, and stomp around. She's angry, she wants everybody to know it, and probably gets some satisfaction in knowing that her behavior is disturbing someone else. There are two different ways of expressing anger through speech. She will either be very loud, dominating the atmosphere; or she will use cold, steely, tense language. Whatever form it takes, we can be sure that her anger is revealed through her speech and/or her actions. Depending on the personality type of the victim, the anger can be expressed overtly (angry outbursts) or subtly disguised (as blame, concern, projection, etc.).

We are all acquainted with the type of person who has such a habit of angry outbursts that he has everyone around him "walking on eggshells," afraid of setting him off. This is overtly expressed anger. We have also been targets of subtle anger, as someone, through clenched teeth, makes a sarcastic remark about us, or angrily blames us for his own misdeed. He may not be shouting, but the words are just as intense and can be just as damaging.

The person with an angry mindset probably has difficulty admitting embarrassment, concern, fear, disappointment, or hurt. Anger is about the only way he can express any emotion. Anger becomes the vehicle for controlling others or circumstances. An angry person knows that others are intimidated by his anger, so it gives him an advantage. It puts him in an offensive position (which also makes him offensive to others.)

There are many negatives associated with this kind of anger. Anger can disrupt the thought processes, as well as impair memory and judgment. The result is irrational thinking and behavior. This principle is illustrated in the life of a man I know whom I have observed for many years. We'll call him "Bob." Bob was a victim in his childhood and still carries his victim status as an excuse for bad attitudes and bad behavior. Little Bob had the misfortune of growing up in a dysfunctional family, where the mother was inadequate in her mothering skills, and the father was often absent. He had no real father figure in his life to give him guidance as to how to be a man. As a child, he became a victim in another way—a victim of circumstances. At an early age he was in a car accident which left him disabled. Very early in his life he was branded a "cripple" because of his physical limitations. Caring for him gave his mother the opportunity to become the self-sacrificing martyr, and she never let him forget it, thus adding guilt to his already shaky self-esteem. Therefore, he became an emotional cripple as well. To add insult to injury, because he was the oldest son in the family, it fell to him to stand in for his absentee father in many ways. Though he was limited physically (only partially lame), as a teenager he was still expected to carry more than his share of the load in taking care of the family. This created resentment in him for many years to come. He grew to despise his mother and eventually became alienated from the whole family.

Although he's had many chances to deal with the reality of his resentment and bitterness and allow God to bring healing and transformation, he has instead chosen denial as a way of existing. Denial can come in two forms:

- Denial that something might have happened at all (past abuse); or,
- Denial that past abuse had a significant impact on the victim.

Either form leads to living a lie. Because a victim is not willing to admit truth, he allows himself to believe all kinds of lies. Being self-deceived, he denies the truth even when confronted with it. This delusion leads to irrational thinking and unpredictable behavior. This condition is bondage, for unless a person is willing to deal in truth about himself and others, he cannot know emotional healing and freedom.

What you will often see in a person like "Bob" is that he has unrealistic expectations (i.e., "Someday my mother will change, and then everything will be all right." Or "I would succeed, if only..."). These expectations allow him to escape personal responsibility by placing blame on others for his condition.

With denial as a frame of mind one is prone to irrational thinking. Others find it difficult to take him seriously, and they tend to reject him. With this rejection, he now has more reasons to consider himself a victim (i.e., "My boss just doesn't appreciate me and what I have to offer.").

Trying to converse with someone in this state can be confusing and frustrating, to say the least. This person seems so intent on protecting and defending himself that his focus is almost always on his own personal agenda. A focus like this causes him to be unable to hear what another is saying if it doesn't relate directly to him and his agenda. This causes him to "re-write history," giving a different account of what happened—an account that is often not true—especially if his account makes him look better or feel better about himself. Unless the anger-based denial is checked, it often grows into unnecessary aggression, in word or deed, which of course damages existing relationships and prevents development of others.

There are some good reasons for an initial angry response to victimization. A person who has been victimized in the past naturally wants to protect herself from further hurt. Her anger can be a method of self-preservation. The anger serves as a protective shield. She thinks that even if she is abused, she can protect her inner self where no one can reach her. In an interview with a woman I'll call Jenny, I heard her story of abuse and how she responded. The following is her story as she tells it:

> He failed me! He was supposed to protect me, and He didn't do it. They told me if I would come to Jesus that He would save me, but nothing is different. Mother still doesn't love me, and Daddy still hurts me. Jesus was the only one left for me to turn to, for everyone else had already failed. I should have known...I should have known that no one would help me! I'll just have to take care of myself, to find a way to protect myself; but I'm so afraid and so alone. What if I fail too? What will I do then? There won't be anyone left.
>
> I really want to run away, but there's no one to whom I can run. Someday I will be all grown up, and then I'll finally be safe. I'll show them all that I don't need their protection or their help! I'll grow up, and then I won't need anyone; and then no one will ever be able to hurt me again!

> Oh no! What am I going to do until I grow up? I know that I can't run away to another place to be safe, but there must be something that I can do. I can't run away, but that doesn't mean I can't go away. There is a place I can go where no one can ever touch me or talk to me or anything else unless I want them to. No one can hurt me inside myself, and that's where I am going.
>
> I'm not going to love any more, and I'm not going to need any more, and I'm not going to ever let anyone hurt me again! I'm safe, but I'm already so lonely that I don't know how I'll be able to stand this emptiness—but I have to. Somehow I have to keep going until I grow up and am big enough to take care of myself. Oh, how I wish I were more than eight years old!

The good news is that this little girl did grow up. As an adult, she discovered that God had not abandoned her as she had thought but had provided the "hiding place" within herself for as long as she had needed it.

Anger is often a secondary emotion in the case of the abused. The first is fright, followed closely by an intense need either to stay and fight or escape in flight. A child who is abused rarely has the option of physically escaping or the ability to fight her attacker. She can't even express her anger at the injustice, for this might bring more abuse. So the anger is suppressed, perhaps for many years, until it rises to the surface and is acted out in negative ways.

Often, the expression of anger gives the victim a channel through which to assert her personal worth—demanding that others respect her. This is reinforced when others give her the attention she craves, even if it is for negative reasons. In this way, she learns that she can get what she wants by throwing tantrums. We are tolerant of a small child if she throws a tantrum, but in an adult it is not a pretty sight! The person with this mindset becomes a bully, and she is more than likely going to become an abuser herself.

An angry mindset is crippling. As I think of the person who has never grown past her anger at injustices done to her, I am reminded of the ancient Chinese custom of foot-binding for women. The process of the practice is described in an internet article reporting on a study done at the University of California at San Francisco in 1997:

> The practice of foot binding began around 960 BC, reportedly to imitate an imperial concubine who was required to dance with her feet bound. By the time a girl turned three years old, all her toes but the first were broken, and her feet were bound tightly with cloth strips to keep her feet from growing larger than 10 cm, about 3.9 inches. The practice would cause the soles of the feet to bend in extreme concavity.[19]

The article further states the devastating effects of this practice, including the prevalence of osteoporosis, foot deformities, inability to squat, and decrease in hip and spine bone density. Such a cruel practice has crippled many generations of Chinese women. Although the practice is outlawed today, the effects of it are still seen in elderly women in China. We Americans rise up in righteous indignation against such practices in other cultures, yet a far more crippling practice runs rampant in our society. This practice is insisting on our "rights" to be angry and to act out in anger. People who choose the anger response as an approach to life are emotionally crippled and suffer long-term consequences of their anger: physically, mentally, emotionally, and socially.

CHAPTER TEN

From Bondage to Freedom

It is easy to see that an angry mindset not only cripples the person who has it but also affects many who come across his path. Anger that is not dealt with becomes a poison, touching all who come into contact with it. There is good news, however, for the person who acknowledges his sinful anger. If he comes to God in confession and repentance, he can experience forgiveness, healing, and freedom. If you are a person with an angry mindset, I urge you to make the choice for healing. God's Word is clear on this matter, for we are commanded: "See to it that no one misses the grace of God and that no bitter root grows up to cause trouble and defile many" (Hebrews 12:15 NIV).

We can learn from the Psalms how to avoid growing the "bitter root" of anger. Psalm 37:8 says, "Refrain from anger and turn from wrath; do not fret—it leads only to evil." It is obvious that this verse is a command, not a suggestion! Just as we have a choice of mindset in the issue of fear, so we have a choice of mindset in the issue of anger. I would like to share with you some approaches that can be taken to overcome an angry mindset.

RECOGNIZE

The first step toward freedom from an angry mindset is to recognize that we have a problem. We need to take an honest look at ourselves and those around us. Let us open our eyes to the toxic effects of unrestrained anger. If you are unsure if you have this problem, I encourage you to ask yourself these questions:

- If you are married, does your spouse "tippy-toe" around you, afraid that the slightest thing will set you off?
- If you have children, are they continually trying to escape being in your presence?
- Do you find that you have difficulty establishing meaningful friendships?
- Are you easily offended?
- Do you think that the world is against you?
- Do you easily blame others for your misfortunes, not recognizing your part in bringing them about?
- Are you easily angered by petty, insignificant things (like having to wait in line or missing out on a good parking space)?

If answered with a yes, each of these questions reveal that you may be in bondage. You are the only one who can choose whether or not you will continue being bound by these chains. The first choice you need to make is to recognize that there is a problem and confess your sin to God (agree with God—He already knows the truth).

READ AND REMEMBER

Recognition, however, is just the first step. If you want to know how to escape from the chains of anger, you must approach God through prayer and Bible study. Read what our Creator has to say to us about dealing with our human sinfulness. There are many wonderful insights in Scripture that can guide us on our earthly journey. It is primarily through prayer and Bible study that I have been set free from a bondage to the past, and I highly recommend this method to all who are still in chains. In reading God's Word we are brought to the place of remembering—remembering the acts of God. God has chosen to involve Himself in human affairs, and the Bible gives us a wonderful panorama of His work in the lives of those who have gone before us. Let me share with you from the Psalms some insights that I have gained. I see some antidotes to the "poison" of anger and what further steps we can take to overcome the angry, victim mentality.

REFRAIN

The first principle is *refraining*. Psalm 37:8 says, "Refrain from anger and turn from wrath; do not fret—it only leads to evil." In this simple verse, I see several principles at work that will be helpful to the person who is trying to find release from the bondage of sinful anger. Refraining from anger suggests self-control. A good place to start is to refrain from speaking angry words. Proverbs 15:1 says: "A gentle answer turns away wrath, but a harsh word stirs up anger." It is hard to have a heated argument with someone if one of the parties refuses to speak in anger. A soft answer is much more powerful than an angry one, for it tends to cause the other person to stop and think, instead of just react.

Refraining from anger means making a choice as to how we respond to offenses. We can choose to react with angry feelings, actions, and words, or we can choose to control our words and actions regardless of what we might be feeling. If we start making a practice of refraining from angry words and actions, after a while a habit is formed and eventually the feelings catch up. This self-imposed restraint causes us to change our perspective and gives us the ability to see things for what they are: the world isn't out to get us; minor offenses don't easily anger us; we don't blame others so readily. We will begin to allow the needs of others to replace our self-focus.

I realize that "refraining from anger" may sound simple, but in actuality we *need* God's power within us to accomplish this. Just as with fear, we need to call upon God to help us, but we must first choose to change. The problem with both angry and fearful victims is the focus on self. We need freedom from our "selves." Choosing to focus on God and His desires for us is very freeing. Hebrews 12:2 admonishes Christians: "Let us fix our eyes on Jesus, the author and perfecter of our faith, who for the joy set before Him endured the cross, scorning its shame, and sat down at the right hand of the throne of God."

When we start focusing (fixing our mind's eye) on Jesus, He will enable us to focus on the needs of others. Jesus walked this earth before us and experienced all the pain of humanity. When abused, He did not lash back with angry words or try to get vengeance on His enemies. Because He was free from anger and bitterness, He was able to minister to many. He even said He "came not to be ministered unto, but to minister, and to give His life a ransom for many" (Mark 10:45). Instead of going the way of man, Jesus chose to obey God. Because He made this choice, salvation is now available to all who accept Him as Savior. The choices we make greatly affect our vertical relationship with God and our horizontal relationships with other people. We must take responsibility for the choices we make, for they have far-reaching consequences. By choosing to give up angry outbursts, we will be able to allow kindness to take the place of anger. If we do this, we will see a great difference in all our relationships.

Another thing can happen when we refrain from anger. We give love a chance. Love has far-reaching consequences, too. In that moment of self-restraint, we can get a different perspective, realizing the other person has needs, too. As we allow love to take the place of anger and resentment, we quickly learn the benefits of such a change—benefits not only to others but to ourselves. I recently ran across an article entitled, "How Love Heals." The article consists of excerpts from a book, *Love & Survival*, by Dean Ornish, M.D. He has some very interesting things to say about how our attitudes and our relationships affect our physical health. He says:

> My work with cardiac patients over the past 20 years has convinced me that love and intimacy are at the root of health and illness. It may be hard to believe that something as simple as talking with friends, feeling close to your parents or sharing thoughts openly can make such a powerful difference in your health. But many studies document that these things do.
>
> Scientists at the University of California, Berkely, studied 119 men and 40 women who were undergoing coronary angiography. Those who felt the most loved and supported had substantially less blockage in the arteries of their hearts. Similarly, researchers in Israel studied more than 8500 men with no prior history of angina (chest pain). Men who had high levels of anxiety were more than twice as likely to develop angina during the next five years. However, those who answered "yes" to the question "Does your wife show you her love?" were significantly less likely to develop angina. I believe the evidence is compelling: love and

> intimacy lead to greater health and healing, while loneliness and isolation predispose one to suffering, disease and premature death.[20]

A victim who is poisoned by an angry mindset may think that relief will come when he can express his anger, but the opposite is true. There is no real relief apart from love and forgiveness. By choosing the path of love and forgiveness, the angry person can finally find peace. He may not know it, but his deepest desire is to have inner peace. Not only does a lack of loving relationships hinder physical healing, but a lack of peace does as well. Addressing this issue, Dr. S.I. McMillen, in his book *None of These Diseases,* states:

> Peace does not come in capsules! This is regrettable because medical science recognizes that emotions such as fear, sorrow, envy, resentment and hatred are responsible for the majority of our sicknesses. Estimates vary from 60 percent to nearly 100 percent. Emotional stress can cause high blood pressure, toxic goiter, migraine headaches, arthritis, apoplexy, heart trouble, gastrointestinal ulcers, and other serious diseases too numerous to mention. As physicians we can prescribe medicine for the symptoms of these diseases, but we can not do much for the under-lying cause, emotional turmoil. It is lamentable that peace does not come in capsules. We need something more than a pill for the disease-producing stresses of the man who has lost his life's savings, the tearful feminine soul who has been jilted, the young father who has an inoperable cancer, the woman whose husband is a philanderer, the distraught teenager with a facial birthmark, and the schemer who lies awake at night trying to think of ways to get even with his neighbor....No one can appreciate so fully as a doctor the amazingly large percentage of human disease and suffering which is directly traceable to worry, fear, conflict, immorality,

> dissipation, and ignorance, to unwholesome thinking and unclean living. The sincere acceptance of the principles and teachings of Christ with respect to the life of mental peace and joy, the life of unselfish thought and clean living, would at once wipe out more than half the difficulties, diseases, and sorrows of the human race.[21]

Given this evidence from the world of medicine that emotions such as anger, resentment, and bitterness can negatively impact on us, it behooves us to "refrain from anger."

REPENT

Not only are we called upon to exercise self-control in situations that may cause us to be angry, but we are also to "turn from wrath." Turning in repentance, then, is the second principle that is seen in Psalm 37:8. Repentance means to have a change of mind.

Unger's Bible Dictionary describes the elements of repentance:

> Repentance contains as essential elements (1) a genuine sorrow toward God on account of sin; (2) an inward repugnance to sin necessarily followed by the actual forsaking of it; (3) humble self-surrender to the will and service of God.[22]

Let us examine more closely the elements of repentance. First, repentance means having a genuine sorrow toward God on account of sin. It is not enough to just say the words, "I'm sorry." It is easy to see in children just how insincere our words can be. Imagine this scene: My granddaughter Lauren is playing with her brother Luke in the game room. They are having a good time jumping on a small trampoline—until Luke decides to push Lauren off the trampoline onto the floor, where she lies in a heap. Not a bone is broken, but feelings are very bruised, which prompts Lauren's cry to her mother—"Mommy, Luke pushed me." Mommy then comes to soothe her daughter's feelings and makes Luke apologize. Can't you just hear him (with all the sarcasm a four-year-old can muster) say, "S-o-r-r-y." Do you think he is sincere? It's doubtful, right?

We tolerate this behavior and attitude in young children because we know that they are just learning how to interact with others. However, when an adult acts the same way, we know that he is exhibiting immaturity, and we just want to say, "Grow up!" God looks at us as His children. How displeased He must be when we are insincere and mouth empty words. Later in chapter 38:18, David demonstrates concisely what sincere sorrow for sin is: "I confess my iniquity; I am troubled by my sin." He does the same thing in other Psalms, such as 51:1-5:

> Have mercy on me, O God,
> according to your unfailing love;
> according to your great compassion
> blot out my transgressions.
> Wash away all my iniquity
> and cleanse me from my sin.
>
> For I know my transgressions,
> and my sin is always before me.
> Against you, you only, have I sinned
> and done what is evil in your sight
> so that you are proved right when you speak
> and justified when you judge.

Do you get a sense of David's sincerity? David's attitude is one of true sorrow for sin, for he sees how his sin has hurt God. True sorrow for sin, then, is the first element in true repentance.

The second element is "an inward repugnance to sin followed by the actual forsaking of it." The first element deals with attitude and the second deals with actions. I would even say that the actions probably will not happen unless one has the proper attitude. For if one is truly sorrowful for his sin, he will see all the ugliness of it and how it can poison his whole being. Sin will be so repugnant to him that he will not want to have anything more to do with it. When he comes to this point, then, it is easier to turn and give up the practice of that particular sin.

The third element that Unger lists is "humble self-surrender to the will and service of God." When one is truly sorrowful for sin and turns away from it, a kind of cleansing takes place. All pride and arrogance is gone and the "self" is purified. God takes His rightful place on the throne of his life. God's sovereignty is recognized as the repentant sinner humbles himself before God. It is then that the person can be a clean vessel for God to use for His plan and purpose.

The latter part of Psalm 37:8 admonishes us to "not fret—for it leads only to evil." Here we are given the long view of what sin can do. I think it is important to recognize that our sins, misdeeds, failures, faults of character, and bad choices have a lasting impact. Unresolved anger will not only impact on others but will have devastating effects on the angry person as well. Psalm 73:18-22 illustrates well this concept:

> Surely You place them on slippery
> ground;
> you cast them down to ruin.
> How suddenly are they destroyed,
> completely swept away by terrors!
> As a dream when one awakes,
> so when you arise, O LORD,
> you will despise them as fantasies.

When my heart was grieved
and my spirit embittered,
I was senseless and ignorant;
I was a brute beast before you.

These verses show what happens to the unrepentant, but what about the one who does genuinely repent? What is the result? Verses 23-26 shed light on this:

Yet I am always with you;
you hold me by my right hand.

You guide me with your counsel,
and afterward you will take me into glory.

Whom have I in heaven but you?
And earth has nothing I desire
besides you.
My flesh and my heart may fail,
but God is the strength of my heart
and my portion forever.

God changes the heart. You might say He is in the business of giving heart transplants. When we come to Him in humility and sincerity, He plants in us His heart. It is important that we see the long view of what our sin (in this case anger) does to others and what it does to us. In this way we can have a "God's-eye" view and having this view will help us give up the angry mindset that has become so destructive.

RECONCILE

Recognizing the fact that we have been a negative influence on others and have caused harm to others should lead us to the next step in getting rid of toxic anger. There is the need to be reconciled. Reconciliation with God occurs when we confess our sins, repent of them, and receive God's forgiveness. Reconciliation with other people can occur when we go to them, confess our sin (offense) against them, and ask for forgiveness. This act needs to be done under God's direction and with great sensitivity. This is where prayer comes in. Ask God to bring to mind the ones who have been hurt by your angry words and actions and then obey Him in seeking their forgiveness. There are many wonderful benefits that can come to the one who is willing to be reconciled to others, as Psalm 133:1 emphasizes: "How good and pleasant it is when brothers live together in unity!" The New Testament gives us further instruction on being reconciled:

Therefore, if you are offering your gift at the altar and there remember that your brother has something against you, leave your gift there in front of the altar. First go and be reconciled to your brother; then come and offer your gift (Matthew 5:23-24).

> Forgive us our debts,
> as we also have forgiven our
> debtors (Matthew 6:12).

> For if you forgive men when they sin against you, your heavenly Father will also forgive you. But if you do not forgive men their sins, your Father will not forgive your sins. (Matthew 6:14-15)

> Therefore, if anyone is in Christ, he is a new creation; the old has gone, the new has come! All this is from God, who reconciled us to himself through Christ and gave us the ministry of reconciliation. (2 Corinthians 5:17-18)

> Therefore *confess* your sins to each other and pray for each other so ***that you may be healed*** [emphasis mine] (James 5:16).

"So that you may be healed" stands out to me in this last verse. Many victims are seeking to be healed, but they are clueless when it comes to God's antidotes for the emotional toxins that invade their souls. We have in this verse a most important principle—that of confessing our sins to one another. Wow! Just think of the implications if Christians took this principle seriously. If we would put into practice this simple command, we could watch the river of forgiveness flow throughout the Body of Christ. People would be free from holding grudges, from engaging in angry outbursts, and from manipulating others for self-serving purposes. The result would be unity in the Body and joy in the Lord.

Forgiveness is like a two-sided coin in that it has two aspects. We have examined the aspect of seeking forgiveness (from God and others), and we recognize that this can bring great release from bondage. However, the flip side of the forgiveness coin is forgiving others. Examine again these verses:

> Therefore, if you are offering your gift at the altar and there remember that your brother has something against you, leave your gift there in front of the altar. First go and be reconciled to your brother; then come and offer your gift. (Matthew 5:23-24)

We all want to be forgiven for our lapses and sins, but how many of us find it easy to forgive another? Giving forgiveness to one who has hurt us badly is almost impossible, but it is an impossibility that God makes possible for those of us who are His. In an article in a state Baptist newspaper, William H. White gives a definition of forgiveness: "Genuine forgiveness is demanding. It is not a thin veneer patched over a relationship but an inner change of heart toward those who hurt us."[23]

Forgiveness is hard work, and most of us are afraid of it.

When someone victimizes us, our natural reaction is to hold a grudge, thinking that somehow the victimizer is being punished by our reaction. However, this is not the case. The one who hurt us probably is not even aware of how much pain he caused. This is particularly true of someone who abused us in the distant past. Our lack of forgiveness is not hurting the perpetrator of the offense so much as it is hurting us. Again, Mr. White states:

> When we fail to forgive we lose something of ourselves. Arnold Lower spoke of anger and an unforgiving attitude: "It is like a draft of poison which burns us up. Anger means to hurt someone, but in reality it is a dagger pointed at our own hearts ... When we grow angry, so many things happen. We cannot eat; we cannot work; we cannot love or be loved. Anger is sheer waste."[24]

We are kidding ourselves and cheating ourselves when we hold on to grudges for the hurts of the past. Forgiveness is absolutely essential if a victim wants to be healed. Forgiveness is probably the primary antitoxin to the poison of anger. The wounded person sometimes is afraid that if he forgives the abuser, the abuser will somehow get away with the abuse and will never be punished. This is where we have to trust God. It is only He Who can mete out the appropriate punishment.

You may say that what was done to you is unforgivable. Many of us have suffered greatly at the hands of others, but I would dare say that few of us have been as wrongly abused as those who were herded off to Nazi concentration camps during World War II. Corrie ten Boom was one of these. She saw great atrocities at Ravensbrück, including the horrible death of her own sister. Could anyone have a reason to hate and to have a desire for vengeance more than she? Yet, she was a Christian and she knew that Christ's followers were commanded to forgive their enemies. Long after the abuse had taken place, Miss ten Boom had many opportunities to speak to large groups of people all around the world. These speaking opportunities provided a platform to give her testimony of how God had seen her through her horrible times of suffering. However, the true test of whether she had forgiven her tormentors did not come until one day she was speaking at a church service in Munich. It was there in that church that she encountered the former SS soldier who had stood guard at the shower room door in the Ravensbruck processing center. She relates her feelings and thoughts at that moment when she met him.

> "Suddenly, it was all there," she recalled, "the roomful of mocking men, the heaps of clothing, Betsie's pain-blanched face. He came up to me as the church was emptying, beaming and bowing. "How grateful I am for your message, Fraulein," he said. "To think that, as you say, He has washed my sins away!" His hand was thrust out to shake mine. And I, who had preached so often ... the need to forgive, kept my hand at my side. Even as the angry, vengeful thoughts boiled through me, I saw the sin of them. Jesus Christ had died for this man; was I going to ask for more? "Lord Jesus," I prayed, "forgive me and help me to forgive him." As I took his hand the most incredible thing happened. From my shoulder along my arm and through my hand a current seemed to pass from me to him, while into my heart sprang a love for this stranger that almost overwhelmed me. And so I discovered that it is not on our forgiveness anymore than on our goodness that the world's healing hinges, but on His. When He tells us to love our enemies, He gives, along with the command, the love itself."[25]

Just as Miss ten Boom was challenged to forgive in an almost unforgivable situation, we are called upon today to rise to the challenge of forgiving. I had an experience years ago when my ability to forgive was challenged. I remember in great detail how I was hurt, the time that I spent in depression, and ultimately coming to the Lord for healing. At that time I was leading a women's Bible study group in my church (not teaching, but coordinating). It was my responsibility to promote the study, to sign up teachers on various topics, and to facilitate prayer and discussion time. I took my responsibility seriously and felt I was in the center of God's will. The years I spent in this leadership position were a great training ground for life. At this time in my life, though, I did not have a lot of self-confidence and was particularly sensitive to criticism. I was generally well liked, however, so I really did not consider that there might be those in the group who would oppose me. As it happened, there were two women in the group who decided I wasn't "Spirit-led" in my leadership, so they took it upon themselves to correct me. They accused me of quenching the Holy Spirit, but other than that they were rather vague in pointing out what it was I was doing wrong. I was baffled as to what I could be doing wrong, and hurt in the way these two ladies went about confronting me and turning others against me. The situation got out of hand and after several weeks of soul-searching, I decided it would be best if I resigned. I felt I had been unjustly accused and was the victim of spiritual abuse.

The criticism resulted in my going into a months-long depression, causing me to question my relationship with God and His will for me. I had felt I was doing God's will in leading the group but was not mature enough to be objective and know how to receive criticism. It was some time before I actively participated in church functions again. The wound went deeply into my heart, and for a time I had to struggle with whether or not I could forgive these women who had taken away my ministry (or so it seemed at the time). I was so afraid I would mess up somehow, so I held back from contributing any service. The day came, however, with the help of my husband and a friend who stood by me that I was able to get a clearer picture of the whole incident. As I came to this realization, I was able to forgive the women. It was after I had forgiven them (though they did not come to me asking forgiveness until two years later) that I became free to minister again in the ways in which God had called me.

There it is in a nutshell. We who have been forgiven by God for our sins must forgive others of theirs. We cannot do this in our own power. The power to forgive comes from God, but we must choose to forgive. Like Corrie ten Boom we will not experience the power to forgive until we reach out our hands to those who have hurt us.

CHAPTER ELEVEN

Poison: Bitterness

Another possible response of victims is that of using their victim status as a tool for manipulation. In this kind of victim, we can see both the fear response and anger response at work. This combination of fear and anger, I believe, creates bitterness.

The fear response is expressed in insecurity and low self-esteem. The abused finds it hard to believe that people will reach out to him with a sincere desire to help. He feels he doesn't merit such devotion. So, in order to receive love and help from others, he manipulates them, getting them to reach out to him because of some obvious need. In this way he gives himself permission to receive their love and help. This pattern of behavior can be seen in someone who is disabled, for example. (This is not to say that everyone who is disabled is in this category.) Being disabled makes him an object of special attention. Others make special accommodations for him and out of compassion go out of their way to help. But he doesn't really feel worthy of their care. So even if he were somehow cured, it would be difficult for him to give up his "reason" for receiving the attention he so desperately needs. It seems to this person that he can only have his needs met if he is "special."

For the person who bases his sense of worth on what others do for him, it is a frightening thought to give up his "specialness" (i.e., handicap). He asks within himself, "Will people still pay attention to me if I'm not disabled? Can I make it in this world as a normal, average, ordinary, functioning human being?" If he answers these questions with a "no," then it is unlikely he will give up his handicap, whatever it may be, even if he had a choice.

The handicap can be physical, mental, or emotional, and it has the power to keep a person from wholeness if he feels he is benefiting in some way by clinging to it. An incident that happened in Jesus' life and ministry on earth gives us a look at someone who can be an example for us. The incident is recorded for us in John 5:1-15. Jesus had an encounter at the Pool of Bethesda in Jerusalem with a man who had been lame for thirty-eight years. This man was waiting for someone to put him in the healing waters of the pool. Jesus picked out this one man from many who were awaiting healing. Verses 6-9 and 14 especially intrigue me.

> When Jesus saw him lying there and learned that he had been in this condition for a long time, He asked him, "Do you want to get well?" "Sir," the invalid replied, "have no one to help me into the pool when the water is stirred. While I am trying to get in, someone else goes down ahead of me." Then Jesus said to him, "Get up! Pick up your mat and walk." At once the man was cured; he picked up his mat and walked.

Later Jesus found him at the temple and said to him, "See, you are well again. Stop sinning or something worse may happen to you." The healing was available, but the man had to make a choice to accept the healing, giving up his victim status. At first he made excuses (verse 7), but then the moment of truth came when Jesus confronted him with the challenge to make the choice for healing. In other words, Jesus urged him to take personal responsibility in coming out of a lifetime of victimhood. This man's whole identity was tied up with his disability. Happily, the man made the choice for the healing that would give him a new identity. In this case, the man was cured as he obeyed Christ's command to "Get up! Pick up your mat and walk" (verse 8).

Of course, he had an even greater healing take place as well—his inner healing. Jesus said to him, "Stop sinning or something worse may happen to you." I think the suggestion here is that his spiritual disease was far worse than his physical one. It would have been a tragedy had the man refused to act on Christ's command to get up and walk, and an even greater tragedy had he refused to obey Christ in regard to his sin. The healing only came when the man exercised faith in and obedience to Christ. He could have continued making excuses and living his life as a victim. There are always some benefits to being a victim if one can manipulate others because of it.

Many choose the "easy" way out when confronted with their lack of personal responsibility. They remain victims because they get some benefit from that way of life. A person who uses his victim status as a tool to manipulate others is a person who is still imprisoned by his past.

This, of course, is not limited to the physically handicapped. Many of us are handicapped in other ways, and we too can become manipulators if we blame others for our victim status. I remember seeing two children once in a race—not an official one—just for fun. The younger of the two children could see that he wasn't going to win, so he tripped and fell, seemingly on purpose. This gave him a reason for losing. He handicapped himself, instead of putting forth the extra effort it would take to beat the older child legitimately. Unfortunately, many adults indulge in similar self-handicapping maneuvers in order not to take responsibility for their failures and inadequacies.

I said earlier that I believe that this kind of behavior rises out of a fear/anger response to abuse. Fear is at the heart of insecurity. Anger is at the heart of bitterness. This is evident in one who has the attitude, "the world owes me." Usually, victims cannot punish their abusers, so they take out their vengeance on others—expecting them to make up for the losses incurred at the hand of a perpetrator of abuse. In part, the anger comes from a sense of injustice. A wrong has been done, and someone should pay. This sense of injustice and feelings of anger will cause a victim to be ever demanding that his rights not be violated, and to be constantly looking for someone to blame for every offense, whether serious or petty. This is the kind of person who frequently talks about suing someone (and sometimes actually does), regardless of what he might have done to bring on the offense. This kind of attitude may benefit civil suit lawyers, but it is not a happy way to live. The mother of "Bob" from my earlier example has lived her life in this unhappy state. She has alienated everyone in the family, but plays on their guilt to get them to do what she wants.

A person with this deep-seated anger and bitterness finds himself trapped. He must see to it that someone is punished because of the sins of abuse against him. He can never be satisfied, though, because it is impossible for others to pay the price demanded by that kind of justice. I think that this kind of person could not be satisfied even if his own abusers were brought to judgment, because he has a lifetime pattern of basing his sense of worth on how others respond to him. This is a very difficult pattern to break, and many people surrounding the victim will be affected.

The fear/anger response is bondage, just like the fear response or anger response. The only way out of this bondage is to trust God to carry out justice against the abuser, to forgive the abuser, and to accept personal responsibility in our relationships with others. We will expand on this in a later chapter.

In the United States we have tolerated unacceptable behavior coming from victims because of the inadequacy of secular psychology to call people to personal responsibility. In an article by Laura Schlessinger in *Reader's Digest*, the author speaks of this problem:

> The modern-day "out" or excuse for such behaviors is generally psychological: 'Considering my hurts, disappointments and traumas, I can't be responsible for the havoc I wreak in the lives of others or the mess I've made of my own life....' After listening to people's stories for almost two decades, I have concluded that the path to healthy relationships and self-respect starts with the decision to do the right thing. Bonnie, 30, wrote to me about her repeated childhood molestations by both a stranger and a family friend, her parents' divorce when she was six and the poverty that kept her from college. "Under these conditions I could have become a victim," she concluded. "But I chose to change my circumstances through hard work and perseverance. While some of my decisions were indirectly related to what happened in my childhood, I am still responsible for the choices I made." Once we decide to make the best of whatever our situation is, we will be better people, and the world will be a better place in which to live.[26]

In an Ann Landers column, a reader who had been raped and beaten by a mentally ill uncle writes:

> When I was 24, I killed a man and was sentenced to life in prison. My state of mind at the time was definitely unbalanced. I actually believed the man I killed was my uncle, and I thought I was acting in self-

> defense. ...I am 42 now, and my struggle for justice goes on.[27]

In the matter of asserting our rights, we Americans have developed this into an art and our society struggles for balance. We live in a very secularized culture that places man at the center of the universe. Individual rights are being shouted about, demonstrated for, and shoved down our throats without regard for what might be for the greater good of society. Even within the church, Christians have taken up the rallying cry for the individual, espousing views from secular psychology that it would be better to avoid.

I recently attended a church women's conference in which there were many different workshops to attend. One that drew my interest was a workshop on anger. At this workshop the leader passed out some materials, including a "Personal Bill of Rights." Forty rights were listed, which seems like a lot to me, but then I've never just listed everything I think I might have a right to. What struck me in reading over this long list was the focus on self and the authority one can give himself to make demands on others. Some examples (my paraphrase) from the list include:

- I have a right to recognize and accept my own value system as appropriate.
- I have a right to determine and honor my own priorities.
- I have a right to all of my feelings.
- I have a right to be angry at someone I love.
- I have a right to make decisions based on my feelings, my judgment or any reason that I choose.
- I have a right to be happy.
- I have the right to be attractive.

In response to this so-called "Bill of Rights" I feel compelled to ask: Who gave us these rights? Where does God's sovereignty fit into the picture? Isn't this just adopting the world-view of secular humanism? It seems to me that a person with this kind of mindset is expecting everyone around him to accommodate him, and it gives him an excuse for "acting out" in anger at the least provocation because someone might be abusing his "rights." After all, it's his right, right? Wrong!

It is my belief that God does not give us all these self-centered rights. It is sad to me that the church, at least in some communities, is not only encouraging people to deal with their problems in a worldly way, but is also not giving a clear message on how to deal with them in a godly way.

There is a godly way to deal with the fear/anger response to abuse. It is possible for the bitter person to rid himself of bitterness and allow God to change the bitterness to joy. In the next chapter, let us look at how this can be done.

CHAPTER TWELVE

From Bitterness to Joy

Ridding oneself of the poison of bitterness can occur when one makes the choice to ask God to change his heart. In this way, one can personally experience God's grace, and he will be better able to give grace to others, particularly those who have wronged him. As Max Lucado says in his book, *In the Grip of Grace*:

> Where the grace of God is missed, bitterness is born. But where the grace of God is embraced, forgiveness flourishes....Hatred will sour your outlook and break your back. The load of bitterness is simply too heavy. Your knees will buckle under the strain, and your heart will break beneath the weight. The mountain before you is steep enough without the heaviness of hatred on your back. The wisest choice—the only choice—is for you to drop the anger. You will never be called upon to give anyone more grace than God has already given you.[28]

The journey to healing for the bitter person is very akin to that of the one who is trying to find deliverance from toxic anger. If a person will follow the counsel of Scripture as stated in previous chapters, he will certainly find the antidote for fear, anger, and bitterness. When a person has recognized his sin, repented of it, and has been reconciled to God and others, he experiences freedom and has much reason for rejoicing. I would even venture to say that the act of rejoicing itself will rid you of any last traces of a fearful or angry mindset. Just as praise serves as an antidote to fear, so it can also be an antidote to anger and bitterness.

David, in the great confession of his adultery with Bathsheba, goes through the steps I have mentioned. Although for a period of time he tried to deny his sin, when confronted by the prophet Nathan, he went on to confess and repent. In Psalm 51 we see David's heartfelt plea for forgiveness, giving us a model to follow when we miss the mark of God's standards. After he confesses his sin, recognizes God's sovereignty, and asks for forgiveness and cleansing, he asks for joy.

> Let me hear joy and gladness;
> let the bones you have crushed
> rejoice. (verse 8)
>
> Restore to me the joy of your salvation...(verse 12)
>
> O LORD, open my lips,
> and my mouth will declare your
> praise. (verse 15)

King David, the one who wrote so many joyful psalms of praise, longed for joy within. I have felt this same longing when I have come to realize that I have strayed from God. For me, fear tends to replace joy when I am depressed. For others, their anger prevents joy from filling their hearts. We can replace the pain within us with joy if we only obey. What one of us does not desire this? It seems to me that holding on to anger, out of pride or other reasons, is so foolish when we can have joy instead. Let us get rid of the poison of bitterness and be able to say with the Psalmist, "This is the day the LORD has made; let us rejoice and be glad in it" (Psalm 118:24).

It is so important for victims to stop blaming others and start looking realistically at their own sinful choices. No one escapes sinning (Romans 3:23 — "for all have sinned") and we know that God knows our sin. God desires that we think and live in truth (Psalm 51:6), so it is necessary to look "in the inner parts" to see our sin as well as our hurts. If we do this with God's guidance He can "teach us wisdom in the inmost place."

So here we are back at choices. Living in victory is a choice. We need our minds renewed, replacing fearful, angry, and bitter mindsets. As we set our minds on God and His plan for us, we can begin the renewal process. When we look above, see ourselves as God sees us, realize the victory in Jesus that we can have in this life and the glory in the next life, our minds are renewed. Colossians 3:9-10 says, "...you have taken off your old self with its practices and have put on the new self, which is being renewed in knowledge in the image of its Creator." So, looking above allows me to see the Big Picture—how each individual life fits into God's plan's for His creation.

Another thing that we can see by looking above (to God) is His view of sin and the sinfulness of man. Colossians 3:5-9 outlines for us a list of evils, the consequences of practicing evil, and the judgment of God against evil. In this passage, we can see a clear picture of a holy and just God, who will not allow sin to rule. God hates sexual immorality, impurity, lust, evil desires, greed, and idolatry. He also warns us to put away such sins as anger, rage, malice, slander, filthy language, and lying. If we practice these sins, we will not only have our minds on things below but will be blinded from seeing things above. I am reminded of a visual aid I once used when teaching a Bible study group. On a poster I drew a picture of a wall of windows. Each window had a pull-down shade, positioned at different levels in each. The shades were black and when pulled down block out the light. The windows represent our lives; the light coming through the windows is the Light of God; and the shades represent sin. The Light is always there, ready to shine through the transparent windows, allowing the room inside to be enlightened. But when we sin, it's as if we choose to reach up and pull down the darkened shade on that one window. Of course, the result is dark shadows cast across the room. The ones inside the room (those who are watching us) are kept from the light and its benefits. We darken our lives by choosing to sin and we block out the Light for others, resulting in their being in darkness as well.

As God's people we are "chosen, holy and dearly loved" (Colossians 3:12a). Because we are chosen, we must choose to "clothe (ourselves) with compassion, kindness, humility, gentleness, patience, forbearance, forgiveness, love, unity, peace, and gratitude" (verse 12b). If I am setting my mind on things above, then I am free to exhibit these qualities. Second Corinthians 3:18 says, "And we, who with unveiled faces all reflect the Lord's glory, are being transformed into his likeness with ever-increasing glory, which comes from the Lord, Who is the Spirit." To me, having an "unveiled face" means being transparent—not hiding behind a false persona. God has freed me from the "persona" I used to hide behind. I have come to understand that when I have been disobedient to God I have taken on a veil myself—a veil of fear, anger, and jealousy. There have been times when I rejected God's light, so I became vulnerable to darkness. This veil became a barrier between God and me. The veil is taken away when I am seeking to be obedient.

I can see how some might not receive the unveiled Christian—the reflected glory of Jesus, for His glory is light and light dispels darkness. Many want to cling to darkness and are unwilling to allow God's light to shine on them. This is illustrated by Moses' encounter with God on Mt. Sinai. "When Aaron and all the Israelites saw Moses, his face was radiant, and they were afraid to come near him" (Exodus 34:30). In Jesus' day, many did not receive Him, even though He was *the* Light from God. Many chose to live in darkness rather than give themselves by faith to the Messiah God had so lovingly sent.

> God is light; in Him there is no darkness at all. If we claim to have fellowship with Him yet walk in the darkness, we lie and do not live the truth. But if we walk in the light, as He is in the light, we have fellowship with one another, and the blood of Jesus, His Son, purifies us from all sin. (1 John 1:5-7)

If we want to live in truth, and have fellowship with the Father and fellow believers then we must choose to "walk in the light." This makes the Christian journey exciting and joyful! God regularly gives me new opportunities to practice walking in the light, and new truths are learned on the way. This principle sheds a new light on trials and suffering that we experience in this life. Hebrews 5:8 states, "Although He was a Son, He learned obedience through the things which He suffered." For me, though I'm not sinless like Christ, I too have learned obedience through my suffering. I found out the cost of disobedience as well. It means broken fellowship and absence of joy.

Bitterness is like a thief that robs a person of joy. It is just impossible to be both bitter and joyful at the same time! When David prayed that God would restore the joy of His salvation, he knew from experience what he was missing. He longed to have joy again. Psalm 92:1-5 expresses the joy David had felt when he wasn't in the darkness of unconfessed sin:

> It is good to praise the LORD
> and make music to your name,
> O Most High,
>
> to proclaim your love in the morning
> and your faithfulness at night,
> to the music of the ten-stringed lyre
> and the melody of the harp.
>
> For you make me *glad* by your deeds,
> O LORD;
> I sing for *joy* at the works of your
> hands.
> How great are your works, O LORD,
> how profound your thoughts!

In a previous chapter, I had much to say about the value of praise in overcoming fear and anger. The principle is the same for those poisoned with bitterness. The more we praise God for His blessings to us and for who He is, the more we will develop a grateful heart. A grateful heart is better able to receive the joy that God wants to give us. For those of us who have experienced and are experiencing God's healing, we have much reason to praise Him. As a matter of fact, we are commanded to praise Him. Psalm 107:20-22 speaks of those who had experienced God's healing power:

> He sent forth his word and healed
> them;
> he rescued them from the grave.
> Let them give thanks to the LORD for
> his unfailing love
> and his wonderful deeds for men.
> Let them sacrifice thank offerings

and tell of his works with songs of
joy.

Recognizing and acknowledging the sovereignty of God and His work among us are the first steps to embracing a grateful spirit. There will be times when we do not feel grateful—times when we tend to focus on the negative things in our lives. However, as we begin to speak words of gratefulness to the Giver of all that is good, our hearts will "catch up" and begin to feel grateful. If you are bound up by bitterness, I recommend an exercise for you. Begin by opening your mind and heart (even if you don't feel grateful) and begin to read aloud some of the following Psalms.

Shout for joy to the LORD, all the
earth.
Worship the LORD with gladness;
come before Him with joyful songs.
Know that the LORD is God.
It is he who made us, and we are
his;
we are his people, the sheep of his pasture.

Enter his gates with thanksgiving
and his courts with praise;
give thanks to him and praise his
name.
For the LORD is good and his love
endures forever;
his faithfulness continues through
all generations. (Psalm 100)

You turned my wailing into dancing;
you removed my sackcloth and
clothed me with joy,
that my heart may sing to you and not
be silent.

O LORD my God, I will give you
thanks forever. (Psalm 30:11-12)

Then will I go to the altar of God,
to God, my joy and my delight.
I will praise you with the harp,
O God, my God.

Why are you downcast, O my soul?
Why so disturbed within me?
Put your hope in God,
for I will yet praise him,
my Savior and my God. (Psalm 43:4-5)

Shout with joy to God, all the earth!
Sing the glory of his name;
make his praise glorious! (Psalm 66:1)

Other passages from Psalms that will be beneficial and encouraging are Psalm 135, 136, 138, 144-150. If you make a practice of reading these and internalizing the truth found therein, you will make a good beginning in replacing bitterness with joy. Another benefit of reading aloud God's Word is that Satan, our enemy, cannot stand to be in the presence of praise that is directed toward God. Satan would have you continue in the bondage of bitterness, but if you have Jesus Christ living within you, you have the power to resist Satan. So—sing out! Satan will flee (see James 4:7), and he'll take the ball and chain of bitterness with him!

When you practice praise, you are practicing the presence of God, for He has promised that He inhabits the praises of His people. God desires that we have joy, and He has given us the formula needed to obtain joy. He has also given us the power to obtain joy through the work of His Holy Spirit. Joy is promised to those who:

- are righteous (Proverbs 10:28)
- promote peace (Proverbs 12:20)
- the ransomed of the LORD (Isaiah 51:11)
- obey (*His*) commands (John 15:10-11)
- fix (*our)* eyes on Jesus (Hebrews 12:2)
- face trials (James 1:2)
- rejoice in the LORD always (Philippians 4:4)

Finally, Philippians 4:8 sums up the kind of choice we need to make if we are to experience joy: we must think on good things—in other words, renew our minds.

> Finally, brothers, whatever is true, whatever is noble, whatever is right, whatever is pure, whatever is lovely, whatever is admirable—if anything is excellent or praiseworthy—think about such things.

When you make the choice to practice God's presence with a grateful heart, focusing on the blessings that are yours and the source from which they come, you will find that the "root of bitterness" in your heart will be transformed into joy. Instead of a bitter tree growing bitter fruit, you will be like the tree in Psalm 1:

> Blessed is the man
> who does not walk in the counsel
> of the wicked
> or stand in the way of sinners
> or sit in the seat of mockers.
> But his delight is in the law of the
> LORD,
> and on his law he meditates
> day and night.
> He is like a tree planted by streams
> of water,
> which yields its fruit in season

> and whose leaf does not wither.
> Whatever he does prospers.

I believe that in this analogy the river represents God's Holy Spirit. God does the planting—He chooses us and gives us salvation and begins His life within us. Through His Spirit, we are nourished and enabled to make our choices—choices that lead to joy. What are these choices? There are some things we must choose not to do:

- Do not "walk in the counsel of the wicked."
- Do not "stand in the way of sinners."
- Do not "sit in the seat of mockers."

Let us examine these choices. What do they mean when we apply them to our daily lives? Notes from the *NIV Study Bible* expand on the meaning of each of these "don'ts." It is thought that there is a progression here—one in which a person progressively associates with the ungodly and participates in their ungodly ways. "Walk in" can be interpreted to mean "order his life according to." "Counsel" indicates deliberations and advice received from another. "Stand" means to station oneself. "Sinners" refer to "those for whom evil is habitual, for whom wickedness is a way of life." To "sit" is to settle oneself, and "mockers" are "those who ridicule God and defiantly reject his law." So, what does this mean to us? Let's paint a possible scenario. A person who is immature in his faith will be attracted more easily to what the world has to offer—let's call it peer pressure. Perhaps a young person is invited to a party. All his friends are going and it sounds like it will be a lot of fun. As he listens to his buddies talking about how great it's going to be, he sees mainly the positives that he can receive if he participates—social status, popularity with the "in" crowd, a date with a really pretty girl, a way to exert some independence, etc. Of course, his friends don't point out the downside—consequences from drinking too much, no adult supervision, unintended romantic involvement, being faced with hard decisions that will have far-reaching results. At first he just listens ("walks in the counsel of the wicked") as he walks along with them. At this point he is indicating to others that he is willing to be influenced by them. Different possibilities are discussed, and then it comes time for a decision—to commit to going or not. Now he "stands in the way of sinners." He "stations himself" before them, indicating they have his undivided attention. They have put out the bait and now they wait for him to take it. If he says "yes" to their invitation, he takes the bait without realizing he will also be hooked. He will find himself now "sitting in the seat of mockers." At first it was not apparent that this group of friends might be "mockers *(of God)*." But should he give an indication that he thinks there's a possibility of immoral activity, he will quickly learn that these so-called friends will indeed mock God and anyone who tries to follow Him. At this point it is very difficult to back down from a "yes" decision, so he is caught—hook, line, and sinker! Do you see the progression? He has gone from just walking along and listening to actually becoming a participant in their activities.

God gives us repeated warnings against even entertaining an idea of sinning. If a person has the power of God within him, he can choose not to even start the process of walking, standing, and sitting with the wicked. Instead of being easily swayed by the opinions of others, he stands tall and strong against the forces of evil. I believe this Psalm (1) is recorded for us for a reason. God wants us to wake up to the fact that we need to make right choices all along the way—choices about things that may appear harmless in themselves, but could lead us astray. The person who is a follower of God and wants to live according to His ways needs to be alert to these choice-making opportunities. We need to make the right decisions from the very beginning of an encounter with temptation.

Now, let's take this same person who may be weak in his faith, but is trying to do what is right. Psalm 1:1-3 points out the benefits that will come to the one who has made the right choices: "Blessed is the man who does not…." The term "blessed" implies happiness. This happiness is the deep-down joy of a believer who is following God's path.

> But his delight is in the law of the
> LORD,
> and on his law he meditates day and night.

The person who loves God and His Word will be able to make the right choices with confidence, because He knows the promises of God. (Incidentally, he will not have time for worldly activities and he will not be satisfied by them.)

> He is like a tree planted by streams
> of water,
> which yields its fruit in season
> and whose leaf does not wither.
> Whatever he does prospers.

Verse one features what the wise person does not do. Verse two features what he does do. By meditating on God's Word, the faithful person learns how to know God and to love Him. God is recognized as his source of joy. There is nothing that can compare with the satisfaction and joy that a person receives when He walks with the Lord. The relationship with God that produces joy is the chief benefit from making right choices, and there are other benefits as well. The person who is walking with God is promised:

- "He is like a tree planted"—God plants in him

the seed of salvation, giving him a stability that will help him weather the storms of life.

- "by streams of water"—For the New Testament Christian "streams of water" can represent the Holy Spirit. God promises the person who chooses His ways that they will be empowered and guided by His Spirit.
- "which yields its fruit in season"—The one who is walking with God in joy will want to share this joy with others. Others will come to know of God's offer of salvation when his children give witness to the power of God in their lives.
- "and whose leaf does not wither."—I believe God promises the faithful that he will have a ministry to others—his "leaf" is ever alive.

If I were to classify this particular tree whose leaf does not wither I would have to say that it is an evergreen. Others will benefit from the shade of the tree, finding in it a shelter. The one who is following God, delighting in His Word, sharing the good news of salvation, becomes a haven for "withered" souls, offering them comfort and peace.

- "Whatever he does prospers."—This is the overall promise of God to those who seek after Him and live in obedience to Him, showing that they have made the right choices in life.

CHAPTER THIRTEEN

Plight of the Abuser

The victim who does not adequately deal with his response to abuse is in danger of becoming an abuser himself. Many, if not all, abusers were once victimized themselves. This abuse can take many forms: physical abuse (violent behavior), verbal abuse (harassment, criticism, blaming, etc.), emotional abuse (making others feel badly), and even spiritual abuse (spiritual leaders abusing their authority).

The fact that victims often become abusers is borne out by the statistics related in a newspaper article entitled, "Justice paints bleak picture of jail inmates."

> Forty-eight percent of female inmates and 13 percent of jailed men have been abused sexually or physically at least once in their lives, according to a profile of the nation's local jail inmates released Sunday. More than a quarter of the women—27 percent—and 3 percent of men said the abuse included rape. Large numbers of the inmates grew up in single-parent homes. "The tragedy is that people who have been victimized often become victimizers themselves," said Eric E. Sterling, president of the Washington-based Criminal Justice

> Policy Foundation. "It's a cycle we could break, but it involves some expense. As a society, we haven't put our resources there."[29]

I think it is time for us as a society to "put our resources there." This cycle of generational abuse can and must be broken if we are to save future children from this curse. "Society" can do nothing, however, unless individuals are willing to change. This is why this book is being written — to encourage people to change.

One example of physical abuse is sexual abuse, which can stem from sexual addiction. Referring to sexual abuse as an addiction, Beth Sterling states in her book, *The Thorn of Sexual Abuse*:

> There are many addictive ways that people use to escape their internal pain, isolation, lack of trust, secretiveness, loneliness, tension, insecurity, and emotional problems. It (sex addiction) also provides them with a false sense of power. Sex addicts are searching for something that cannot be found in their addiction—emotional and spiritual security.[30]

What then is the plight of the abuser, or victimizer? Can he change? What are the risks to himself if he chooses not to change? There are many manifestations that a person is an abuser, other than the exhibited abuse. For, you see, the victimizer also brings much harm to himself. The fact that someone might be an abuser may not be obvious to all. We might expect that victimizers come from only certain socioeconomic groups or thoroughly pagan people or the criminal element in society. However, this problem is insidious. It has found its way into the best neighborhoods, is common in every race and creed, and even surfaces from time to time in the church.

In a previous chapter we listed symptoms associated with victims. What are some symptoms, or warning signs that we can associate with victimizers? One list of signs comes from an Ann Landers column:

1. Jealousy of your time with co-workers, friends and family.

2. Controlling behavior. (Controls your comings and goings and your money and insists on "helping" you make personal decisions.)

3. Isolation. (Cuts you off from all supportive resources such as telephone pals, colleagues at work and close family members.)

4. Blames others for his problems. (Unemployment, family quarrels—everything is "your fault.")

5. Hypersensitivity. (Easily upset by annoyances that are a part of daily life, such as being asked to work overtime, criticism of any kind, being asked to help with chores or child care.)

6. Cruelty to animals or children. (Insensitive to their pain and suffering, may tease and/or hurt children and animals.)

7. "Playful" use of force in sex. (May throw you down and hold you during sex. May start having sex with you when you are sleeping or demand sex when you are ill or tired.)

8. Verbal abuse. (Says cruel and hurtful things,

degrades and humiliates you, wakes you up to verbally abuse you or doesn't let you go to sleep.)

9. Dr. Jekyll and Mr. Hyde personality. (Sudden mood swings and unpredictable behavior—one minute loving, the next minute angry and punitive.)[31]

In *The Thorn of Sexual Abuse*, Beth Sterling quotes from *Out of the Shadows*, by Patrick Carnes. He describes the experience of sexual addiction as progressing through a four-step cycle, which intensifies with each repetition:

1. Preoccupation—the trance or mood wherein the addicts' minds are completely engrossed with thoughts of sex. This mental state creates an obsessive search for sexual stimulation.

2. Ritualization—the addicts' own special routines which lead up to the sexual behavior. The ritual intensifies the preoccupation, adding arousal and excitement.

3. Compulsive sexual behavior—the actual sexual act, which is the end goal of the preoccupation and ritualization. Sexual addicts are unable to control or stop this behavior.

4. Despair—the feelings of utter hopelessness addicts have about their behavior and their powerlessness.[32]

Sexual abuse is certainly a form of victimization that has some of the most far-reaching consequences. However, we must not neglect to examine other kinds of abuse as well, for when we include verbal abuse, emotional abuse, and spiritual abuse, we rattle the scars of most of the population. I believe we are all victims to some extent and probably most of us have engaged in some form of abusive behavior. However, for this writing I want to emphasize the chronic abuser—one who has chosen a lifestyle that victimizes others.

As I said, I believe that all of us have been victimized in our encounters with other people as we have journeyed through life. Some abuse has been severe and it's obvious to us that we are victims. However, there are more subtle forms of abuse. One of these is verbal abuse.

There is an old saying that many of us grew up with: "Sticks and stones may break my bones, but words will never hurt me." Do you believe that this is true? I don't. We know that a person can heal from broken bones and other physical ailments, but victims of verbal abuse have no treatments available to them in the form of medical intervention. There is no magic pill we can take that will ease the throbbing pain in our hearts when we receive unwarranted criticism from others. There is no soothing salve to apply to the wounds in our souls that are the result of poisonous words of slander or false accusation. There is no surgery available to cut out the bitterness and resentment that grow like a cancer within us when we are the objects of ridicule. The words of an abuser have as much sting to the soul as bullets do to the body. The victimizer often knows he has power over another through the words he speaks. With our words we have the capacity to give blessing or cursing. A verbal abuser places curses on others that are as binding as hexes from hell. How many of us are in bondage to the harsh words spoken to us in anger by our parents? Much of how we feel about ourselves stems from what was said to us and about us when we were children.

Children have a great need for affirmation and praise and words of encouragement from their parents, but for many there is little positive reinforcement. Abusive words are not always angry words. As a matter of fact, verbal abuse can take several forms. Some examples are: profanity, cursing, criticism, sarcasm, harassment, blame, and guilt-projection.

In the home in which I grew up, the verbal abuse would not have been obvious to the casual observer. It was subtle. It came in the form of criticism and lack of praise. My mother was a godly woman and did the best she could to rear me, but she had been harshly criticized by her father and had never gotten over it. In ignorance she passed on to her children a critical spirit by her words. Since my mother worked outside the home from the time I was about 10 years of age, it became my responsibility to do much of the housekeeping and meal preparation. I was obedient and did the best I could, but it seemed my best was never good enough. Upon arriving home, my mother would overlook the things I had done right and immediately point out something I had done wrong or had omitted doing. Growing into adulthood I carried with me feelings of inadequacy and incompetence which, in part, were programmed into me by my mother's criticism. Even after I married, it was a long time before I got over the feeling that I couldn't do anything right. So, even what some might call a very mild abuse can have long-term negative results. For instance, I have heard it said that it takes nine compliments to outweigh one criticism. Is it any wonder that there are so many people who never believe in themselves enough to really succeed in life?

Sometimes abuse can also come in the form of neglect. Do we not victimize our children when we neglect them, not attending to their very basic needs? This area of neglect is widespread in our society. One example is that of neglectful fathers—fathers who have abdicated their responsibilities in child-rearing and in many cases have withheld emotional support as well as financial support. There is an epidemic in our land that will impact on children for many generations to come. That epidemic is fatherless homes. In a book entitled *Life Without Father* author David Popenoe says:

> The decline of fatherhood is one of the most unexpected and extraordinary social trends of our time. In just three decades—1960 to 1990—the percentage of children living apart from their biological fathers roughly doubled to 36 percent. By the turn of the century nearly 50 percent of American children may be going to sleep each evening without being able to say good-night to their dads. Most of today's fatherless children have fathers who are perfectly capable of shouldering the responsibilities of fatherhood.
>
> A surprising suggestion emerging from recent social-science research is that it is decidedly worse for a child to lose a father in the modern, voluntary way than through death. The children of divorced and never-married mothers are less successful by almost every measure than the children of widowed mothers. Men are not biologically attuned to being committed fathers. Left culturally unregulated, men's sexual behavior can be promiscuous, their paternity casual, their commitment to families weak. The decline of fatherhood is a major force behind many of the most disturbing problems that plague our society. [Some of these are] prevalence of sexually active teenagers; teen suicide, alcohol and drug abuse. [Also] Scholastic Assessment Test scores declined 75 points between 1960 and 1990. The absence of fathers seems to be one of the most important causes of these trends.
>
> On the face of it, there would seem to be at least one potentially positive side to fatherlessness: without a man around the house, the incidence of child abuse might be expected to drop. Unfortunately, reports of

> child neglect and abuse have skyrocketed since 1976. One of the greatest risk factors in child abuse, investigations found, is family disruption, especially living in a female-headed, single-parent household. Explanations include poverty and the fact that children receive less supervision and protection from men their mothers bring home. Children are also more emotionally deprived, which leaves them "vulnerable to sexual abusers, who commonly entrap them by offering affection, attention and friendship," wrote David Finkelhor, an expert on child abuse.Another group that has suffered in the new age of fatherlessness is, of course, women. Fatherlessness appears to be a factor in generating more violence against women. Partly this is a matter of arithmetic. As the number of unattached males in the population goes up, so does the incidence of violence toward women.[33]

The statistics above demonstrate graphically the effects of abuse upon an entire society. If one could observe an abuse situation, one would tend to think that the victimizer has the upper hand and is controlling the victim. It appears that there is a victim and a victor, but the fact is the abuser is not a victor, or winner. Both the victimizer and the victim are losers. The abuser's "victory" is short-lived, for he will suffer from his behavior as much, perhaps, as the one he victimizes. For, you see, the victimizer is a sinner, and he is acting out of his sinful nature. There are consequences that any of us suffer when we sin. These consequences can come in the form of physical symptoms and psychological problems, can have social implications that are far-reaching, and can break our fellowship with God. Let us look closer at the unrepentant victimizer and what he is like. Psalm 10:2-11 gives an apt description:

> In his *arrogance* the wicked man hunts
> down the weak,

who are caught in the schemes he devises.
He boasts of the cravings of his heart;
he blesses the greedy and reviles the LORD.
In his pride the wicked does not seek him;
in all his thoughts there is not room for God.
His ways are always prosperous;
he is haughty and your laws are far from him;
he *sneers at all his enemies.*
He says to himself, "Nothing will shake me;
I'll always be happy and never have trouble."
His mouth is full of curses and lies and threats;
trouble and evil are under his tongue.
He lies in wait near the villages;
from ambush he *murders the innocent,*
watching in secret for his victims.
He lies in wait like a lion in cover;
he lies in wait to catch the *helpless*;
he catches the helpless and drags them off in his net.
His victims are crushed, they collapse;
they fall under his strength.
He says to himself, "God has forgotten;
he covers His face and never sees."

• The italized words in this passage show the attitude of the victimizer. It is common for the chronic abuser to be arrogant, prideful, greedy, irreligious, and deceitful. He first deceives himself. The chronic abuser can always find "reasons" for his behavior, and will often try to justify or rationalize it in his own mind. Some examples of excuses of a sexual abuser come from *The Thorn of Sexual Abuse*, by Beth Sterling:

- I'm simply providing sex education for her. After all, she has to learn sometime.
- Since she didn't say no, she must want to do it.
- It's okay because she looks and acts older than she really is.
- I'll only do it this one time—it won't hurt her—she'll soon forget all about it.
- I've tried, but I'm a weak person and just can't help myself![34]

These excuses came from research done with sex addicts, but the rationale is not limited only to sexual abusers. The description of an abuser from the Psalms was given from the perspective of a man who had been victimized. From the victim's point of view, it seems that the victimizer does indeed have an upper hand and is allowed to get away with the abuse. However, again I assert that the abuser suffers too. In the preceding Psalm, we see one who is arrogant and does not acknowledge his wrongdoing. This does not mean, however, that he actually "gets away with it." God judges all sin and there is a price to pay for arrogantly continuing along the wrong path.

This same David, who wrote from the victim's perspective, was also a victimizer at one time. We know of his bad decision to engage in adulterous behavior with Bathsheba, and for a time went on as if he would not have to suffer consequences for that behavior. However, in Psalm 38 and others, we discover the personal suffering he endured before he came to repentance. In these Psalms, we can see what his unconfessed sin did to him with regard to physical suffering, psychological and spiritual anguish, as well as the social ramifications of his actions.

Physical Symptoms

Psalm 38:

Because of your wrath there is no
health in my body;
my bones have no soundness
because of my sin. (Verse 3)

My wounds fester and are loathsome
because of my sinful folly. (Verse 5)

I am bowed down and brought very
low;
all day long I go about mourning. (Verse 6)

My back is filled with searing pain. (Verse 7)

My heart pounds, my strength fails
me;
even the light has gone from my
eyes. (Verse 10)

For I am about to fall,
and my pain is ever with me. (Verse 17)

Psalm 32: (AMP)

When I kept silence [before I confessed],
my bones wasted away
through my groaning all the day long. (Verse 3)

For day and night
    your hand [of displeasure] was heavy upon me;
my moisture was turned into the drought
    of summer. (Verse 4)

It is obvious from these verses that a person who engages in abusive behavior will suffer physically. David's sin was adultery. Could it be that he suffered from some venereal disease, perhaps? This could certainly be one of the consequences of his behavior. But it could also be that his troubled spirit led to physical symptoms. In our present age, we know from medical research as well as personal experience that stress is a prime culprit in producing a great variety of ailments.

Impelling evidence that stress leads to physical ailments is shown in a study done by a Dr. Kawachi of Harvard University: "Two 1994 studies showed that men with high levels of anxiety were at four to six times the risk of fatal heart disease than men who had no symptoms."

Not only does the abuser bring great physical pain on himself, he spreads the pain to others. This can be seen especially in those who are sexual abusers. A newspaper article entitled "Straying husbands, lovers spread cervical cancer" in my local paper bears this out:

> Unfaithful husbands may give their wives cancer. That's the conclusion of a study that found women are five to eleven times more likely to develop cervical cancer if their men frequent prostitutes or have many sexual partners. The cancer is directly linked to human papilomavirus, or HIV, a virus that is commonly spread by sexual intercourse. "Although the study showed that men brought the virus home to their wives, any woman can put herself at increased risk by having many different sexual partners," said Dr. Keerti V. Shah, a professor at the Johns Hopkins University

School of Medicine.[35]

The pain that is spread to others is not limited to sexual abuse, of course, but evinces itself in other ways, such as in physical beatings and misuse of drugs. We have all seen the devastation and wreckage in people's lives who use and abuse mind-altering drugs. If we don't know someone personally with this problem, we can certainly be aware of it through the news media and the entertainment industry. This fact was brought home to me several years ago as I became acquainted with Michael, a precious baby of four months of age. Visiting in the home of his foster parents allowed me the opportunity to observe the disastrous effects of a pregnant mother who had abused drugs. He had been taken from this mother and placed in a foster home with the hope that he could overcome these effects and be able to live a somewhat normal life.

Michael was just 6 weeks old when he came into the Clawson* home. The baby boy had been born to a woman of age thirty-five. This was her fourth child, but she couldn't keep him. She had had problems keeping her other three as well. She was a cocaine addict, and her life was out of control. Michael is only one of thousands of victims of such irresponsible behavior on the part of expectant mothers.
The foster parents who took him into their care temporarily had the tremendous job of creating a normal child out of this piece of damaged humanity. The first three weeks were especially difficult, for Michael had to be on "de-tox" drugs to help him withdraw from his mother's curse. He cried and screamed a lot when he was between doses. The Clawsons poured their love into the boy, with large doses of affection and words of affirmation. Still, it took three weeks before they could even begin to feel he was bonding with

* Name is changed to protect privacy

them, for only then would he look at them. From research that the foster parents had done, they came to understand just how handicapped little Michael was. Undoubtedly brain-damaged, it was impossible for him to develop normally. Since he had little muscle tone, even his motor skills were affected. It was almost as if they were trying to breathe life into a rag doll. Much patience was needed, and perseverance—much more than with a normal newborn.

Little Michael was a victim in the truest sense, having no choice in his birth circumstances. He entered this life with more than three strikes against him, all because of an abusive mother. Do you think this mother suffered any because of what she had done to her children? I am certain that she suffered greatly. The abuser in any situation will at the very least suffer from guilt.

We human beings have within us the capacity for feeling guilt when we do wrong. This guilt feeling is placed there by God in order to lead us to repentance. Unfortunately, many abusers do not want to deal with their guilt in the right way, so in an attempt to escape guilty feelings, a whole host of psychological and spiritual difficulties arise. We have observed the physical effects the abuser suffers. Now let us look again to the Psalms to see what's going on in the mind of an unrepentant abuser.

Psycological/Spiritual Difficulties

- Weighed Down With Guilt

Psalm 38:

...your arrows have pierced me,
and your hand has come down upon me. (Verse 2)

My guilt has overwhelmed me...
like a burden too heavy to bear. (Verse 4)

I am bowed down and brought very
low;
all day long I go about mourning. (Verse 6)

I am feeble and utterly crushed.
I groan in anguish of heart. (Verse 8)

All my longings lie open before you,
O Lord;
My sighing is not hidden from you. (Verse 9)

- Paranoid

Those who seek my life set their traps,
those who would harm me talk of my
ruin;
all day long they plot deception. (Verse 12)

Many are those who are my vigorous
enemies;
those who hate me without reason are
numerous. (Verse 19)

- Fear of Lost Reputation

Do not let them gloat
or exalt themselves over me when
my foot slips. (Verse 16)

- Depression

For I am about to fall,
and my pain is ever with me. (Verse 17)

...I am troubled by my sin. (Verse 18)

Psalm 6:6

I am worn out from groaning;
all night long I flood my bed with
weeping
And drench my couch with tears.

- Fear of Abandonment

Psalm 38:21

O LORD, do not forsake me;
Be not far from me, O my God.

These burdens of guilt, paranoia, fears, and depression that we see in the life of the Psalmist are evident in present-day abusers as well. Beth Sterling, author of *The Thorn of Sexual Abuse* states:

> Because [sexual] addicts judge themselves..., they live with constant guilt, shame, pain, and fear of discovery. Since they don't trust other people, they have extreme fear and difficulty in establishing honest relationships. Addicts seldom have fun; they don't know how. Fearing disapproval and rejection, a sex addict doesn't follow through on things. Love is frightening to the addict, making him feel powerless. He quickly builds emotional walls—once built, they are not easily torn down.
>
> Addicts are convinced that if people really knew them, they would be rejected.[36]

The burden of guilt is probably the most difficult to deal with. We can deal with guilt in a number of ways. We can be sure, however, that the one who is terrorizing others will not escape judgment even if he tries to deny his guilt. Gwen Shamblin of The Weigh Down Workshop (a Christ-centered weight loss program) says in her seminars that "God created guilt as a result of sin so that He can get our attention and lead us to repentance." She further states her belief that there are basically four wrong ways people respond to guilt, with only one right way to respond. I have paraphrased Mrs. Shamblin's concepts below. The four wrong ways are:

- Anger and blaming others or circumstances. This comes out of an extreme self focus coupled with a great resistance to changing one's self. This angry person is uncomfortable around those who are doing what's right, because it seems his abusive deeds are highlighted. He will often ridicule the "Goodie-two-shoes" for their circumspect behavior. This allows him to take the attention away from his own actions, so that he doesn't feel obligated to justify them. His pattern of coping with guilt involves blaming others, so he doesn't feel responsible for his own actions. This is projection. This kind of person also delights in another's downfall.

- Self-pity—"legalized pout." The one who is prone to feel sorry for himself is headed for depression. He is caught in a trap—he doesn't want to change his behavior, but he wants the pain of the guilt to go away. This sets up a cycle of self-pity and guilt which leads to more sinful behavior.

- Mr. "Fix-it Fox"—thinks he can fix the problem himself. This person seems very self-sufficient and tends to think that he can tackle any problem. He knows he has a problem, but by trying to fix it himself he becomes fatigued and stressed out. This leads to more guilt.

- Denial of guilt—Some in our society would lead us to believe that there is no such thing as guilt. This is false comfort, however, for the truly guilty.

The only right way to deal with guilt is to confess wrongdoing and repent. The one who refuses to acknowledge his guilt and continues in his abusive behavior will also continue to suffer from unexplained physical ailments and mental anguish. Dr. Henry Brandt, family counselor, speaker, and author, corroborates this truth in his book, *The Heart of the Problem:* "Human emotions can totally disengage our brain, preventing rational behavior and acceptance of the fact that we sin. I have seen this in my own life and in those of my clients."[37]

In addition to physical symptoms and various psychological difficulties, for the compulsive abuser, there is impaired social interaction. This is evident in the relationships that the abuser has. He is alienated from society and creates enemies among those whom he has abused. As we look back at Psalm 38, we can see this truth:

- Alienation

> My friends and companions avoid me
> because of my wounds;
> my neighbors stay far away. (Verse 11)

- Enemies-Real and Imagined

> Those who seek my life...talk of my
> ruin. (Verse 12)

> Many are...my enemies;
> ...those who hate me without reason. (Verse 19)

- Inability to Communicate

> I am like a deaf man, who cannot
> hear,
> like a mute, who cannot open his
> mouth. (Verse 13)

This verse says the abuser becomes like a deaf and mute man, which indicates that this is a process. As the sinner continues to reject God and is unrepentant, it becomes harder to hear God speak. His communication with others also becomes unfruitful, incoherent, and deceitful, which further alienates people. His relating to others is seriously hampered and he becomes locked in bondage, unable to give or receive love. Remember the example of Bob given in the previous chapter? He is far along in this process of becoming "deaf" and "mute." Many conversations with him are confusing and one never knows if he's telling the truth.

- Low self-worth

> Those who repay my good with evil,
> slander me when I pursue what is
> good. (Verse 20)

Others are suspicious of this person because they have observed (and perhaps been the victim of) his pattern of abusive behavior. Eventually, even when he occasionally does what's right, it is hard for people to give him credit. Motives are questioned and one is never sure whether the person is doing what's right just because it is right or because of appearances.

Another kind of abuser is one who controls others through spiritual abuse. According to Ken Blue, author of *Healing Spiritual Abuse,* a definition of spiritual abuse is: "deliberate exploitation and domination of the weak by a grandiose, authoritarian spiritual dictator."[38] He further states:

> Almost any kind of abusive behavior may be found at this level: threats, intimidation, extortion of money, demands for sex, public humiliation, control over private lives, manipulation of marriages, elaborate spying and similar practices. When psychologically and spiritually weak people fall under the control of a narcissistic demagogue, there is potential for great harm to all.[39]

It is somewhat obvious to the average person that fringe groups are abusive, but unfortunately, spiritual abuse is not limited to cults. It is found among misguided spiritual leaders even in mainline denominational churches. And their victims are legion. Many of these victims come from very fundamentalist backgrounds, but instead of getting a balanced picture of God (i.e., a God of love and justice), they are led to see God only as a severe judge who demands perfection in thought and deed. These victims' parents and other authority figures in the church used God and the Bible to threaten and control them. The perpetrators of this kind of abuse are usually self-appointed authorities. Mr. Blue refutes this kind of authority:

> Truth and its authority are not rooted in a personality or office. It is derived from the Word of God and the gospel it proclaims. I concur with Michael Horton, who maintains that there is no such thing as "The Lord's Anointed," preachers who are above the Word.... Any claim to divine authority for commands, expectations, revelations, or guidance that are not stated in the pages of Holy Scripture are marks of a spiritual tyrant and Pharisee.[40]

According to Blue, other evidences of spiritual abuse are an overemphasis on tradition, a "no talk" rule that forbids talking about certain subjects, an exaggerated desire for honor and titles, and last but not least, legalism. It is intriguing to me that a person can become a spiritual abuser. Mr. Blue shares the testimony of one man who came out of that bondage:

> A friend who is a repentant (sic) spiritual abuser told me how he became one. He described his childhood as "religious but void of acceptance or approval." When he left home, he searched for a place where he could feel significant. He also wanted a job where people needed him. He gravitated to the professional Christian ministry (an all too common story). He explained how in his first church he quickly gathered about him those parishioners who met his needs, those who supported him uncritically. "In time," he said, "I established a class system, with my supporters at the top and those who posed a threat to my leadership at the bottom. This system aided me in the delusion that I was doing the right things." My friend then told me the pain and destruction he inflicted on those at the bottom and how he trained those at the top to follow his abusive style. He was finally delivered from his compulsion to control others by a deeper understanding of God's mercy and grace. He has now publicly repented and is seeking to undo the damage.[41]

This man's story not only shows how he came to be a spiritual abuser, but also demonstrates how abuse is handed down from one generation to another. Do you think this man was happy as long as he was abusing others? Do you think that he was happy as a child? Had he not been victimized by the lack of approval of his parents, would he have become an abuser of others? I suspect that this kind of abuse had been going on for several generations, he came to the place where he saw all the destruction, and then finally he chose to put an end to the cycle of abuse.

What can motivate an abuser to give up his abuse of others? No matter the type of abuse (physical, sexual, verbal, emotional, or spiritual), it is when he wants to stop his own pain that he is motivated. Whether the pain is from a sense of guilt or shame, or he suffers from physical ailments, or he is alienated from others and has low self-worth, he wants to escape the pain. I believe this is why God allows us to suffer the consequences of our sin—so that we will come to the place where we are desperate for peace and recognize that He is the only One who can bring about our healing and freedom from bondage.

There is bad news and there is good news. The bad news is that if an abuser does not make the choice for healing, the cycle of abuse will continue to succeeding generations. The good news is that the cycle can be broken as both the victim and the victimizer seek healing from The Great Physician—God. In the next chapter we will see how healing can come to the one who makes the choice for healing.

CHAPTER FOURTEEN

Pathway to Healing

This matter of healing the victim and the victimizer can appear to be a tangled web at times. There are many in our modern world who claim to have the means for untangling the web, thus hoping to stop the cycle of generational abuse. Let us examine some of the worldly advice that is prevalent, but first look at God's admonition to the Christian. Romans 12:2 states: "Do not be conformed any longer to the *pattern* of this world, but be transformed by the renewing of your *mind.* Then you will be able to test and approve what God's will is—His *good, pleasing, and pleasant* will" (italics mine). This verse prompted me to think about some of the "patterns of this world"—to identify them and to contrast them with God's patterns for us. A pattern can be very difficult to change. The "pattern of this world" means the worldly (carnal) way of thinking. There are many forces at work trying to determine our mindset. These forces lead us away from God and into death (estrangement, darkness, confusion, rebellion), as Romans 8:6-7 says: "The mind of sinful man is death, but the mind controlled by the Spirit is life and peace; the sinful mind is hostile to God."

- Worldly Patterns

What are some of the world's patterns and how do we guard against developing these patterns for living? The first pattern that came to my mind was a *preoccupation with self*, evidenced in some of the popular phraseology of our day:

- *My* rights
- *My* feelings
- What's in it for *me*?
- If it feels good, do it.
- Do *my* thing
- Assert *yourself*
- *You* deserve a break today
- *I'm* worth it
- Love *yourself*
- *Self*-actualization
- *Self*-esteem

There's even a magazine entitled *Self*. All these oppose Christ's instructions to us:

- Deny yourself... (Luke 9:23)
- Love is not...self-seeking. (1 Corinthians 13:5)
- Fruit of the Spirit...self-control. (Galatians 5:23)
- Let us be self-controlled, putting on faith and love. (1 Timothy 5:8)
- ...self-controlled so that you can pray. (1 Peter 4:7)
- Be self-controlled and alert. (1 Peter 5:8)
- Fits of rage, selfish ambition, dissensions. [list of sins in Galatians 5:20.]
- Do nothing out of selfish ambition or vain conceit, but in humility consider others better than yourselves. (Philippians 2:3)

- Each of you should look not only to your own interests, but also to the interest of others. (Philippians 2:4)
- ...offer your bodies as living sacrifices. (Romans 12:1)
- Whoever wants to save his life will lose it. (Matthew 16:25)

From our focal passages in Psalms, the desire of the Psalmist is stated in chapter 119:36: "Turn my heart toward your statutes and not toward selfish gain." Psalm 119 contains 176 verses that celebrate the benefits of knowing God's laws, or precepts. We are admonished not to follow the world's patterns of thinking, and we are instructed in how to replace these patterns with godly patterns.

- Success-seekers

Another worldly "pattern" is attaining wealth, fame, prestige, knowledge, popularity, etc. These things are symbols of *success* to the worldly mind. However, God says:

> Seek ye first the Kingdom of God and His righteousness and all these things shall be added unto you. (Matthew 6:33 KJV)

> Humble yourselves therefore, under God's mighty hand, that He may lift you up in due time. (1 Peter 5:6)

> Not by might nor by power but by my Spirit, says the LORD Almighty. (Zechariah 4:6)

> Do not wear yourself out to get rich. (Proverbs 23:4)

> Charm is deceptive, and beauty is fleeting. (Proverbs 31:30)

> ...but the worries of this life, the deceitfulness of wealth and the desires for other things come in and choke the Word, making it unfruitful. (Mark 4:19)

> I urge you, brothers, to watch out for those who...by smooth talk and flattery they deceive the minds of naive people. (Romans 16:17-18)

> Do not deceive yourselves. If any one of you thinks he is wise by the standards of this age, he should become a "fool" so that he may become wise. For the wisdom of this world is foolishness in God's sight.(1 Corinthians 3:18-19)

> Do not love the world or anything in the world. If anyone loves the world, the love of the Father is not in him. For everything in the world—the cravings of sinful man, the lust of his eyes, and the boasting of what he has and does—comes not from the Father but from the world. The world and its desires pass away, but the man who does the will of God lives forever. (1 John 2:15-17)

The choice is ours. We can live according to the patterns of this world, risking not only our earthly lives but our eternal security as well. We need to choose God's patterns if we are to know freedom, healing, and victory. What is God's idea of success? Joshua 1:8 gives us a clue: "Do not let this Book of the Law depart from your *mouth*; *meditate* on it day and night, so that you may be careful to *do* everything written in it. Then you will be prosperous and successful." Note the words in italic print. These emphasize the arena in which God's precepts operate:

- The mouth—affecting what we *say*. What does your vocabulary consist of? Your words will reflect what is in your heart. Remember that one of the most powerful ways to overcome negative speech is to replace it with positive speech, particularly praise (as discussed in chapter six).

- Meditate—what we *think.* What do you find yourself thinking about most of the day? Here is another choice we have to make. We can dwell on offenses against us and have a brooding mindset, or we can choose to think on good things and the positive qualities of people. The New Testament, in Philippians 4:8, exhorts us: "Finally, brothers, whatever is true, whatever is noble, whatever is right, whatever is pure, whatever is lovely, whatever is admirable—if anything is excellent or praiseworthy—think about such things."

- Do—Doing, of course, is acting. We must choose to behave in such a way as to reflect what God has done in our minds. God transforms our hearts and renews our minds. Our behavior will be a reflection of what has taken place in our hearts. Our "walk" and our "talk" will demonstrate the convictions of our hearts and what God has done in our lives. As we progress on our healing journey, supernatural behavior will become more "natural."

- Knowledge-seekers

A third "pattern" of this world is evident in its *philosophy*. Popular philosophies in today's world include:

- Autonomy—not accountable to the Creator.
- Plurality—accepting all religions as true.
- Democracy—ethics and morality decided by

majority vote, not on absolute truth.

- The natural goodness of man—that we're evolving into superior beings.
- It doesn't matter what you believe as long as you're sincere.
- Survival of the fittest—might makes right.

How does godly philosophy compare with worldly philosophy? The authoritative Word of God says:

> ...It is appointed unto men once to die, but after this the judgment. (Hebrews 9:27)

> He (Jesus) said: "I am the Way, the Truth, and the Life—no man comes to the Father except by me." (John. 14:6)

> There is a way that seems right to a
> man,
> but in the end it leads to death. (Proverbs 14:12)

> For all have sinned and fall short of the glory of God. (Romans 3:23)

> Whoever believes in him [Christ] is not condemned, but whoever does not believe stands condemned already because he has not believed in the name of God's one and only Son. (John 3:18)

> Yours, O LORD, is the greatness and the power and the glory and the majesty and the splendor, for everything in heaven and earth is yours. Yours, O LORD, is the kingdom; you are exalted as head of all. Wealth and honor come from you; you are the ruler of all things. In your hands are strength and power to exalt and give strength to all. Now, O God, we give you thanks, and praise Your glorious name. (1Chronicles 29:11-13)

> He [Jesus] is the image of the invisible God, the first-born of all creation. For by him all things were created: things in heaven and on earth, visible and invisible, whether thrones or powers or rulers or authorities; all things were created by him and for him. He is before all things, and in him all things hold together. (Colossians 1:15-17)

Dear Reader, can you see the contrast between worldly patterns of thinking and acting and the patterns God desires for us? I encourage you today to examine yourself and see how many of the world's patterns you have adopted. Allow God to transform and renew your mind, freeing you to live the abundant life He has in store for all those who obey Him. Replacing worldly patterns of thinking with godly patterns is a process. The Psalms give us some clues as to how to go about this task.

RECOGNIZE

First, it is necessary to recognize that we have need of God's healing touch. The Psalmist pours out his heart before God, recognizing not only his need but the fact that God is the only one who can meet that need. Another passage that shows us that the Psalmist recognized his need is Psalm 77:1-2: "I cried out to God for help; I cried out to God to hear me. When I was in distress, I sought the LORD; at night I stretched out untiring hands and my soul refused to be comforted." Not only did the Psalmist recognize his need, but he recognized God as the Healer who could bring comfort and relief:

> Psalm 43:3-4:
>
> Send forth your light and your truth,
>   let them guide me;
> let them bring me to your holy

mountain,
to the place where you dwell.

Then will I go to the altar of God,
to God, my joy and my delight.

Psalm 56:3

When I am afraid, I will trust in you.

Psalm 57:2

I cry out to God Most High,
to God, who fulfills his purpose for
me.

Psalm 68:5

A father to the fatherless, a defender
of widows,
is God in his holy dwelling.

REMEMBER

Of course, recognizing that we have a need requires remembering. There is much value in remembering our pasts. We look at the past to determine in what ways we might have been victimized. As I have reflected on this I have come to realize that I very seldom advise people to dig up the dirt of their pasts. There are occasions, however, when I might ask a person about his past because of certain attitudes and behaviors that are obviously in his current lifestyle. I never encourage anyone to dwell on his past or to use past victimization as an excuse for present attitudes. In other words, I am not encouraging people to take on "victim" labels, but rather challenging them to give up such labels and take personal responsibility for their current attitudes and actions.

I admit, I was skeptical at first about this healing of memories. I am not one to dwell on the past, and I was not sure that I wanted to know some things I might have forgotten. However, I came to see that sometimes it is helpful to glance backward before we can progress forward in our walk with the Lord. Psalm 43:1-5 illustrates this principle:

> Vindicate me, O God,
> and plead my cause against an
> ungodly nation;
> rescue me from deceitful and
> wicked men.
>
> You are God my stronghold.
> Why have you rejected me?
> Why must I go about mourning,
> Oppressed by the enemy?
>
> Send forth your light and your truth,
> let them guide me;
> let them bring me to your holy
> mountain,
> to the place where you dwell.
>
> Then will I go to the altar of God,
> to God, my joy and my delight.
> I will praise you with the harp,
> O God, my God.
>
> Why are you downcast, O my soul?
> Why so disturbed within me?
> Put your hope in God,
> for I will yet praise him,
> my Savior and my God.

When I look to my past I am not only seeing ways in which I was wronged, but I am also seeing God's grace at work in me, enabling me to forgive those who have wronged me. I also realize that in looking at the past I will see instances when I too have sinned and need to seek forgiveness from God. A personal example of this process is when I realized (in my 30's) that I had developed a pattern of criticism because I had lived with a mother who criticized me without the balance of occasional praise. I chafed under that criticism for many years, but I did not see that I was continuing the pattern myself. As I reflected on this, I asked God's forgiveness for my behavior and was able to forgive Mother for hers. This was very freeing for me and created a heightened awareness of times when I would slip back into the old habits. I determined in my heart that I would not pass down to my children the same kind of negative criticism that I grew up with. I know I haven't always succeeded in overcoming a critical spirit, but I believe our children would say today that they felt affirmed by me in their various endeavors.

For me, the healing journey took place over several years and God spoke to me through many scriptures as I have read and studied His Word as a daily practice. Some verses that I can remember that confirmed in me that I was doing the right thing were:

> Surely you desire truth in the inner
> parts;
> you teach me wisdom in the
> inmost place. (Psalm 51:6)

> Search me, O God, and know my
> heart;
> test me and know my anxious
> thoughts.
> See if there is any offensive way in
> me,

> and lead me in the way everlasting. (Psalm 139:23-24)
>
> You were taught, with regard to your former way of life, to put off your old self, which is being corrupted by its deceitful desires; to be made new in the attitude of your minds; and to put on the new self, created to be like God in true righteousness and holiness. (Ephesians 4:22-23)

This searching of my past was done in a spirit of prayer and under God's direction, for I trusted Him to shine His light on dark places in my memory.

> Everything exposed by the light becomes visible, for it is light that makes everything visible. (Ephesians 5:13-14)
>
> I waited patiently for the LORD;
>   he turned to me and heard my cry.
> He lifted me out of the slimy pit,
>   out of the mud and mire;
> he set my feet on a rock
>   and gave me a firm place to stand. (Psalm 40:1-2)

My main point in all this is that I believe there is value in looking at the past to see what has produced certain responses in us. Many people are still angry and bitter because of what was done to them in the past. Many are fearful. I believe we need to give up the anger and fear that characterize our lives, and trust God to do a work of healing in our hearts. Honesty requires identifying the events of the past and acknowledging the truth of what impact those events had on us. The result should be an adjustment in thinking (renewing our minds) and a change in behavior (no longer acting out in destructive ways). Another consequence of this kind of reflection is seeing God at work, and therefore having more reason to praise and glorify Him.

Another important thing to remember is that we need to trust God's timing for our healing. For me, my memories were veiled and only revealed to me as an adult who could handle the information. True healing cannot come until the pain is acknowledged (i.e., God brings it to the surface). Psalm 40:1 says, "he turned to me and heard my cry." I believe God even hears our silent cries when we don't know what to ask or how to ask. The cry for help may be manifested in different ways: physical symptoms, anger, depression, passive aggression, perfectionism, paranoia, codependency, etc.

> He lifted me out of the slimy pit,
> out of the mud and mire;
> he set my feet on a rock
> and gave me a firm place to stand. (Psalm 40:2)

God showed me that my real foundation was Him. Knowing that my foundation was God Himself affirmed my worth.

> He put a new song in my mouth,
> a hymn of praise to our God.
> Many will see and fear
> and put their trust in the LORD. (Psalm 40:3)

As a singer, this verse is especially significant to me. Singing with great freedom is a marvelous thing! Before I went through my time of inner healing, my singing was different. I was anxious, not very confident, and was afraid of what people thought of me. I was still in bondage to my fears, which gave me a sense of inferiority. I was afraid to be "me" and didn't really think I had much to offer. As I came to an understanding of who I was in Christ, I began to realize that I had worth and that God had given me a message to share through the medium of music. My whole purpose for singing was and is that "many will see and fear and put their trust in the LORD." Let us all, as believers, let this verse be a kind of mission statement for us. In order to be used effectively for God in His Kingdom work, we need to get rid of unnecessary baggage that we carry from the past.

REMOVE GUILT

After we have recognized our need for healing and we remember the past honestly, we need to seek God's forgiveness for our own offenses. This is the only way to remove guilt. Once again, the Psalmist speaks to us:

> My guilt has overwhelmed me
> like a burden too heavy to bear.
>
> My wounds fester and are loathsome
> because of my sinful folly.
> I am bowed down and brought very
> low;
> all day long I go about mourning.
>
> My back is filled with searing pain;
> there is no health in my body.
>
> I am feeble and utterly crushed;
> I groan in anguish of heart. (Psalm 38:4-6)
>
> Do not withold your mercy from me,
> O LORD;
> may your love and your truth
> always protect me. (Psalm 40:11)

Max Lucado says in his book, *In the Grip of Grace*:

> Where the grace of God is missed, bitterness is born. But where the grace of God is embraced, forgiveness flourishes....Hatred will sour your outlook and break your back. The load of bitterness is simply too heavy. Your knees will buckle under the strain, and your heart will break beneath the weight. The mountain before you is steep enough without the heaviness of hatred on your back. The wisest choice—the only choice—is for you to drop the anger. You will never be called upon to give anyone more grace than God has already given you.[42]

The New Testament tells us that "all have sinned and fall short of the glory of God, and are justified freely by his grace through the redemption that came by Christ Jesus" (Romans 3:23-24). Christ bore the burden of your guilt to Calvary and nailed it to the cross so that you can live by grace. Bring your guilt to Him, confess, repent, and receive His forgiveness, and you will see your guilt removed.

Whether the victim has an angry mindset or a fearful mindset, the result is the same—he carries with him much emotional baggage. This emotional baggage needs to be left behind. In my work, I travel a great deal and always have to pack carefully for my journeys. You know how it is: the airport officials only allow you so much carry-on luggage and it has to be just the right size. On one of my overseas trips I had to try to fit what I thought was a carry-on bag into one of those measuring slots stationed at the gate. Guess what? My bag would not fit! So, it was taken from me and sent to be checked. What a bother! These size and weight rules certainly are inconvenient at times, but I realize they are rules that were made with the safety of the passengers in mind.

Just as too much baggage can keep you from flying, so does emotional baggage keep you from progressing on your healing journey. Instead of trying to drag the baggage of anger and fear everywhere we go, let's get rid of it! There is a popular phrase in our current culture: "Lighten up." That is what we need to do! We need to lighten our load if we are going to live victoriously. Lightening of our loads is a process. It comes in stages as we learn more about ourselves and we make the choices that will lead us to our destination: healing. Little by little, God shows us who we are and gives us directions that point the way to His paths of righteousness. In giving up old attitudes and habits we become free to soar through life.

For any journey, preparation is important. If I am going to get on an airplane, I must think ahead what kind of luggage to take and how I am going to pack it. For my healing journey, I must also plan and prepare—in other words, think! We need to examine ourselves closely and allow God to shine His light on our inner selves. This must be the first step in the journey. There is a Chinese proverb that says, "a journey of a thousand miles begins with a single step." Take a step toward God and He will walk with you the thousand miles, or however much distance is required to transform you from being a victim into a victor.

To carry the luggage analogy further, picture yourself at the gate, ready to board the plane. You are allowed two carry-on pieces of luggage. In the spiritual realm, I believe these two pieces of luggage are *faith* and *obedience*. Not only are you allowed these two pieces of luggage on your healing journey, they are required. God says in Hebrews 11:6:

> But without faith it is impossible to please him: for he that cometh to God must believe that he is, and that he is a rewarder of them that diligently seek him. (KJV)

And 1 John 5:3-5 expands on this principle:

> This is love for God: to obey his commands: and his commands are not burdensome. For whatever is born of God overcomes the world. This is the victory that has overcome the world, even our faith. Who is it that overcomes the world? Only he who believes Jesus is the Son of God.

Would you like to be an overcomer? An overcomer is a victor—one who wins in the battles of life. Do you want to leave behind the baggage of fear and anger? Then, you must pick up the two pieces of luggage marked "faith" and "obedience" to begin your journey of healing. Other words for faith and obedience are trust and submission. You cannot hope to fully recover from the abuse in your past without placing your trust in God and submitting to His will.

Sonshine

By B. Kay Coulter

Oh, let the Sonshine shine on me.
Oh, let the Sonshine shine on me.
Oh, let the Sonshine shine on me.
Jesus is the Son—let Him shine on me.
Let the Sonshine in to dry up the tears.
Oh, let the Sonshine in; chase away all the fears.
Bring us out of dark—right into the Light.
Walking straight ahead, unafraid of the night.
We need a lot of Son in our lives to grow.
Jesus is the Son, and He wants us to know
That He can bring us warmth, and a spiritual glow.
He gives us this freely, because He loves us so.
So open up your blinds, and let the Sonshine in.
He'll give you new life, and freedom from sin.
Then you can give the Sonshine that others may live.
It's because of the Son that we have life to give.
Oh, let the Sonshine shine on me,
Oh, let the Sonshine shine on me,
Oh, let the Sonshine shine on me.
Jesus is the Son; let Him shine on me.

CHAPTER FIFTEEN

Breaking the Cycle

When we choose to walk by faith, we choose to believe God's promises—like those found in Psalm 40:4: "Blessed is the man who makes the LORD his trust, who does not look to the proud, to those who turn aside to false gods." God will honor a person who has a humble heart and will "restore the joy of [His] salvation" (Psalm 51:12). Joy comes to take the place of grief as old grudges are removed. Griping turns into gratefulness as we realize the healing that has taken place in our hearts, and we can say with the Psalmist:

> Many, O LORD my God,
>   are the wonders you have done.
> The things you planned for us
>   no one can recount to you;
> were I to speak and tell of them,
>   they would be too many to declare. (Psalm 40:5)

> Let them give thanks to the LORD for
>   his unfailing love
>   and his wonderful deeds for men,
> for he satisfies the thirsty

and fills the hungry with good
things. (Psalm 107:8)

But may all who seek you
rejoice and be glad in you;
may those who love your salvation
always say,
"The LORD be exalted!" (Psalm 40:16)

I am under vows to you, O God;
I will present my thank offerings to
you.
For you have delivered me from
death
and my feet from stumbling,
that I may walk before God
in the light of life. (Psalm 56:12-13)

Sing to God, sing praise to his name,
extol him who rides on the
clouds—
his name is the LORD—
and rejoice before him. (Psalm 68:4)

As your heart overflows with thankfulness to the Great Physician who brings healing, you will have a desire to tell others. A person who has been cured from a deadly disease will be eager to tell others. A person who has been healed of the deadly toxins of chronic fear, anger, and bitterness will also be eager to share the good news of his newly-found freedom. I can almost hear the excitement in the voice of the Psalmist when he says: "I proclaim righteousness in the great assembly…I speak of your faithfulness and salvation" (Psalm 40:9-10). An important principle is seen here—that of openly giving God the credit for your healing. The more you tell others, the more you will realize your healing. It is important to state publicly what God has done for you. Praise Him in your private worship and testify about Him publicly as you share the joy that He has put in your heart. Joy will replace the bitterness that once occupied your heart. Your life will be changed and you will be used of God to influence others.

As you experience God's healing, you will also find that you desire to be with other believers, participating in public worship and ministering to others through the church. You may also experience more healing as you become a part of the Christian community. God does not intend for us to be loners, struggling to make it on our own. The Church was established by Christ to be a haven and support group for believers. We encourage one another as we each embark on our individual journeys. We have prayer support available to us. We have a place where we belong. We get our eyes off ourselves and become aware of the needs of others, and we can be used as healing instruments in their lives. We can share our victories and our failures and know that we are loved unconditionally. When we stumble, God will send our brothers and sisters in Christ to help us up. Do you see how important it is to associate ourselves with an established body of believers? Do not neglect this, for your healing will be incomplete without it.

It is with this strong foundation that you will be able to go on to the next step in the healing process—beyond personal healing. What is beyond personal healing? The next step is taking what you have learned from your experiences and reaching out to others through ministry. I believe we are not placed here in this world just for our own happiness and wholeness. God has a greater purpose for us. Ministry to others who are hurting will help us realize His purposes for us. We will not have to look very far for opportunities to minister, for we are surrounded by those in need of God's love. We can start with our own families.

The Psalms have much to say about our responsibility to pass on the truths of God to future generations. Psalm 71:18 is a good example: "Even when I am old and gray, do not forsake me, O God, till I declare your power to the next generation, your might to all who are to come." Another example of the responsibility and privilege of passing down God's truth to our children is Psalm 112:1-2: "Praise the LORD. Blessed is the man who fears the LORD, who finds great delight in his commands. His children will be mighty in the land; the generation of the upright will be blessed." As we gain confidence in our own standing with God, we will be better able to reach out to those around us. God will bless us as we reach out, as He has promised in Psalm 41:1: "Blessed is he who has regard for the weak; the Lord delivers him in times of trouble."

Psalm 48:12-14 reminds us: "Walk about Zion, go around her, consider well her ramparts, view her citadels, that you may tell of them to the next generation. For this God is our God for ever and ever; he will be our guide even to the end." There are certain eternal principles at work here. Just as God has led us in the past, he will continue to do so in the future. Rehearsing His faithful deeds in our own pasts helps us to be more effective in helping others. What I see in this passage is that Zion, or Jerusalem, becomes symbolic of my life. As I review the ways in which God has been a stronghold (ramparts, citadels) to me, I want to pass on to the next generation the fact of God's faithfulness. Not only do I have the privilege of recounting God's blessings to others, I have the awesome responsibility to "proclaim his righteousness to a people yet unborn" (Psalm 22:31).

The Old Testament speaks of God's deliverance of the children of Israel from Egypt, where they had been enslaved for 400 years. In Deuteronomy, we have recorded for us the commands of God to the free generation of Israelites who would enter the Promised Land. With this freedom came the responsibility to pass on the commands of God to succeeding generations. If the people of Israel were faithful to obey God in this matter, they would be blessed. Deuteronomy 4:9 says,

> Only be careful, and watch yourselves closely so that you do not forget the things your eyes have seen or let them slip from your heart as long as you live. Teach them to your children and to their children after them.

And Deuteronomy 11:18-21 gives us more specific instructions:

> Fix these words of mine in your hearts and minds; tie them as symbols on your hands and bind them on your foreheads. Teach them to your children, talking about them when you sit at home and when you walk along the road, when you lie down and when you get up. Write them on the door frames of your houses and on your gates, so that your days and the days of your children may be many in the land that the LORD swore to give your forefathers, as many as the days that the heavens are above the earth.

The New Testament tells us of freedom from a different kind of slavery—the slavery to sin. Jesus is our Deliverer, and we can know release from bondage by putting our whole trust in Him. As we experience His deliverance, we are compelled to tell others how they too can be free. We become "new creations" (2 Corinthians 5:17). As new creations, we want to share with others our newfound joy. My experience has been that the more we share, the more we realize God's purposes in our lives. God calls us to invest ourselves in others—taking risks, making sacrifices, trusting God to take care of our own needs.

Have you experienced God's healing and deliverance? Have you known His transforming power? Have you come to know God by committing your life to Christ? If so, God has a purpose for you. His purpose for believers can be found in 2 Corinthians 5:17-20:

> Therefore, if anyone is in Christ, he is a new creation; the old has gone, the new has come! All this is from God, who reconciled us to himself through Christ and gave us the *ministry of reconciliation*: that God was reconciling the world to himself in Christ, not counting men's sins against them. And he has committed to us the *message of reconciliation*. We are therefore Christ's ambassadors, as though God were making his appeal through us. (italics mine)

As Christians, we are all called to be ministers—ministers of reconciliation. What an awesome privilege and responsibility! We have peace in our hearts and we can bring peace to others. Remember our Psalm 51 text? In this psalm, David poured out his heart in confession and repentance and pled with God to restore the joy of salvation. He desired to have a clean heart and wanted to begin anew to live for God. Trusting that God would accomplish this restoration in his life, he then goes on to say in verse 13: "Then I will teach transgressors your ways, and sinners will turn back to you." David was able to look beyond personal healing, realizing that there were others who needed God's restorative power in their lives.

How good God is to give us second chances! Even though we sin while we live on this earth, He still has a purpose for us. Let us be like David—repenting, recommitting our lives to God, and obeying God as He leads us to minister to others.

It is not enough to just receive God's healing for ourselves. We must reach out to others who are hurting and introduce them to the Great Physician. The New Testament is full of instances where Christians ministered to others, following the example of Jesus. The apostle Paul was one of God's outstanding examples of one who is a minister of reconciliation, and one who delivered the message of reconciliation. He not only established churches across Israel, Asia, and Europe, but he continued his ministry to them through his return visits and his epistles. He was concerned that the new Christian converts would not mature in the faith, but would remain "babies," only concerned about their own spiritual health. Through letters like the two to the Corinthian Christians, Paul urged the new converts to grow up and discover God's purpose for them. Early in his second letter to the Corinthians (verses 1:3-4), Paul clearly states the call to be ministers of reconciliation:

> Praise be to the God and Father of our Lord Jesus Christ, the Father of compassion and the God of all comfort, who comforts us in all our troubles, so that we can comfort those in any trouble with the comfort we ourselves have received from God.

In becoming ministers of reconciliation, we will begin to have a different perspective on our lives and on the needs of others. We are able to change our attitudes and see how we fit into God's "big picture." God's big picture is like a tapestry. He sees the work of art that our lives are becoming (as if different-colored threads are woven together), and we just see the under-side, with knots and hanging threads. We may have suffered greatly as victims, but we have experienced God's healing. If so, we will desire to stop the cycle of destructive behavior in our families. Hurtful family experiences have far-reaching consequences, as we have seen in the earlier chapters of this book. But God grants us the ability to overcome destructive behavior in our own lives and also will enable us to break the cycle of generational abuse. We do not *have* to perpetuate the sins of our fathers. We can make the choice to free our children from the ruinous attitudes that we have inherited. It is a hard choice, but with God's help we can reverse the trend of abusive behavior in our families.

The attitudes that arose from our responses to victimization (fear, anger, bitterness) need to be changed. There comes a point when we must say, "The buck stops here." I began writing this book after observing my own family of origin. I realized that for some reason my children, in terms of emotional stability, had fared better than the children of my siblings. When I began to ask why this had happened, I remembered the kinds of choices that I had made. I chose not to continue the pattern of destructive attitudes and behavior that I had learned from my parents. I have experienced in my own life how to break the cycle of hurtful family experiences. I have learned that there are some very specific things that we can do to help our children and grandchildren avoid much of the pain of victimization. The difficult part for us, of course, is making the necessary changes in attitude and deliberately changing how we relate to our children. Difficult, but not impossible! I would like to share with you some things I have learned about this process.

The process includes examining what God's Word has to say to us as parents, asking for wisdom, and then choosing to make the necessary changes. The elements of this process are as follow:

- Awareness of our behavior patterns
- Acknowledgment that some of these patterns are destructive
- Reprogramming, or renewing our minds
- Understanding our child's needs

- Encouraging and affirming good attitudes, traits, behaviors
- Changing curse to blessing—replacing negative words with positive ones
- Praying daily, asking for God's wisdom
- Obeying Scripture—spending time with God's Word daily so as to receive instruction. 2 Timothy 3:16: "All Scripture is God-breathed and is useful for teaching, rebuking, correcting and training in righteousness, so that the man of God may be thoroughly equipped for every good work."

When my husband and I were first married, we had the privilege of learning about child-rearing from some study tapes entitled *Know Your Child.* The teacher was a pastor and well-known radio teacher by the name of Dr. Joe Temple, and he resided in Abilene, Texas. The lessons I learned under his teaching became invaluable to me as we started our family. Much of my child-rearing skills came as a result of having learned from this godly Christian man and his teaching from God's Word. Rev. Temple had great credibility, for he had seven children. He even experienced single fatherhood, for his wife died of cancer when she was forty years of age. He had proven the value of following God's Word with his own family. Several things that he taught are still engraved upon my mind even today. He based most of his teaching on Proverbs 22:6, which states in the Amplified Bible, "Train up a child in the way he should go [and in keeping with his individual gift or bent], and when he is old he will not depart from it." There is much richness in this simple, but profound, verse, yet what made the greatest impression on me was the admonition to bring up a child "in keeping with his individual bent." The challenge to me and to all parents is that we know our children well enough to determine what that individual bent is. We need to bring up our children with knowledge and understanding. How do we really get to know our children? By studying them! And spending time with them—quality and quantity time. Our pastor recently told a story about two children and their father. The father realized that he was not spending as much time with his daughters as he wanted to spend. So, he apologized to them. Then he added, "You know, it's not always important the quantity of time we spend together, as it is the quality of time we spend together." The girls, ages six and four, did not understand. So he explained: "Quantity means how much time and quality means how good the time is we spend together. Which would you rather have?" The six-year-old quickly replied, "We want quality time and lots of it!"

That is what children want—time with you, the parent. We as parents must be willing to sacrifice other things (maybe even good things) in order to spend the time with our children that it takes to get to know them. Modern experts tell us that we need to be involved in our children's lives. An article from my hometown newspaper reported on a program given at a local hospital. It illustrates this point:

> Most parents want their children to become successful in life and building self-esteem in a child is an important part of reaching that goal, according to a local educator Susan Carroll. [*Ms. Carroll*] outlined the five steps for building self-esteem in a child. She said it is important to establish a sense of security..., which means knowing what to expect.
>
> The second point in building self-esteem is identity or a self-concept, she said. This includes having an awareness of one's strengths or knowing what they do well.

> Creating a sense of belonging is another important area in building self-esteem. "Being important to others and belonging to a group—to humans—is very important." She said usually in situations that make individuals feel really good, it probably involved someone else in some way.
>
> Another important area is developing a sense of purpose. "This is the feeling of excitement you get when you do something well. You really feel great and that's a sense of purpose."
>
> And the final point Ms. Carroll stressed as being important in instilling self-esteem in children is achieving a sense of personal competence. This area involved providing support and encouragement and recognition.
>
> "Self-esteem comes from valuing yourself," Ms. Carroll said.[43]

A child learns to value himself as he receives signals from his parents about how much they value him. Another article from my local paper, entitled "Hug your children with positive words" states:

> Your children first begin forming an opinion of themselves by the manner in which you talk to them. How they feel about themselves affects all areas of their lives. Is much of what they hear from you positive or negative?
>
> Here are gentle reminders for busy parents from the Virginia Coalition for child abuse which you might find helpful.
>
> - Make ordinary, every day experiences pleasant for your child.

- Set aside special times with each of your children. Allow them to choose an activity they would like to do.
- Catch your child being good and praise the behavior.
- Move physically closer to your children when you talk with them. Hold them.
- When you talk with your children or when they talk with you, stop what you are doing and look into their eyes.
- Remember they are their own person and may do things differently than you.
- Respond to your child with patience and understanding. Scolding or criticizing your child in front of others shows a lack of sensitivity and respect.
- Share your positive feelings with your child, often.
- For a heart-to-heart talk, go to the child's room or to a quiet place.
- Comments such as "That's no big deal" or "You shouldn't feel that way" make your children believe that their feelings are not important to you.
- Through your daily words and actions, let your children know that they can't be replaced, that each is very special to you and that you love and value them.[44]

Many parents do not love and value their children enough to spend time with them. Sometimes this lack of parental attention and willingness to deal with problems results in an over-dependence on doctors to prescribe behavior-altering drugs. An article I read in 1999 entitled, "Drugs not always solution for behavior," bears this out:

> A reaction is under way against drugging children because they are behaving like children, especially boy children. Colorado's elected school board recently voted to discourage what looks like drug abuse in the service of an ideological agenda. The board urged teachers and

> other school personnel to be more restrained about recommending drugs such as Ritalin for behavior modification of children, and to rely more on discipline and instruction.
>
> In 1996, 10 percent to 12 percent of all American school boys were taking the addictive Ritalin. This is due to a growing tendency to regard as mental problems many characteristics that are really aspects of individuality. So pharmacology is used to relieve burdensome aspects of temperament.
>
> The idea that most individuals deficient in attentiveness or confidence are sick encourages what McHugh [*professor of psychiatry at Johns Hopkins*] calls pharmacological "mental cosmetics." This "should be offensive to anyone who values the richness of human psychological diversity. Both medically and morally, encumbering this naturally occurring diversity with the terminology of disease is a first step toward efforts, however camouflaged, to control it."[45]

From another article in the same newspaper, the report was given of a local program, drawing my attention to the fact that whole communities must be involved in helping our children to grow up to be productive citizens instead of victims:

> The need for communities and churches to be aware of "Violence and Child Abuse" was the thrust of talks given...by Bell County Sheriff Dan Smith and Child Advocacy Center Director Michelle Farrell.
>
> Those attending learned about the seven types of child abuse: emotional, physical, sexual, abandonment, negligence of supervision, medical needs or physical necessities to sustain life.
>
> The advocacy center in Central Texas is a non-profit

> organization created to minimize the trauma of child abuse victims and its purpose is to prevent, detect, investigate and treat child abuse. The center includes a multidisciplinary agency of team professionals working together to serve the best interests of the child victims.[46]

An article in a state Baptist newspaper caught my attention with this title, "Child abuse hitting closer to home in Texas." In it, writer Scott Collins quotes Ken Hall, president and CEO of Buckner Baptist Benevolences:

> From a theological point of view, you have to understand the character of God and you have to understand that pain and suffering go to the heart of God's love for people. Jesus made some very blunt statements about the need to care for children. He said that for anyone who would do harm to a child, it would be better if a millstone were tied around that person's neck and thrown in the sea. Christians have an obligation to respond to the problem of abuse and neglect.[47]

What happens to children who do not get their needs met at home? If they are desperate for attention, they will find a way to get it, even if it is in a very negative way. Such is the case with children and young people in our schools today. Over the past few years, our nation has seen a rash of school shootings, where students are shooting other students. We have to question why this is happening. Parents are being confronted with questions about their methods of parenting. Laws have been enacted in an attempt to prevent further violence. Our schools have become armed camps. After a recent shooting incident in San Diego, well-known syndicated columnist Cal Thomas wrote an article in response. In the article, he highlights the need for parental involvement in the lives of their children.

The Associated Press reports that in the wake of the shootings at Santana and Granite Hills High Schools near San Diego, "some frightened parents are demanding tighter security while others are seeking alternative ways to educate their children."

Putting armed security guards inside school buildings might help, as it did at Granite Hills, but at what cost to the idea of what a school should be?

All of these efforts, along with proposals for school vouchers and a different curriculum, might reduce the consequences of poor character development, but government schools cannot heal themselves. No matter how much money is spent, it's ultimately up to parents to decide whether they are willing to invest the necessary time and resources to properly rear their own children. This critical job cannot be done solely by others and it cannot be done as one might cook a microwave dinner.

Numerous studies have shown that modern teens are angry. They have a right to be. They have been abandoned by "no-fault" divorcing parents for whom "love" is more about feelings than commitment. Children feel conditionally loved. If they perform up to parental expectations, they are affirmed. But if they struggle or fail, too many parents refuse to spend the time necessary to set them right. It might interfere with their pursuit of affluence.

We dump our children in day care at ever-earlier ages. Many parents don't have time for much more than checking homework. How many families have unhurried meals together with the television off? How many families see the transferal of their own beliefs and values to their children as their primary responsibility, ahead of school and certainly ahead of culture? How

> many parents ridden with guilt for their failure to properly rear their children, allow them to make their own moral, cultural and relational decisions and are afraid to say "no" to anything a child wants because it might make the youngster angry?
>
> One parent at Granite Hills told AP he was "seriously considering" home schooling his 15-year-old daughter rather than let her return to the school. That father is on to something. He is seeing the intellectual and moral development of his child as his own responsibility, not the state's. He will be making an investment in his daughter, which will likely pay dividends for life.
>
> No child is taught to kill but he has to be taught to love, respect, honor and value, not only his own life, but the lives of his classmates, parents and teachers. He has to experience love and acceptance. He has to know his life has purpose and meaning. No amount of money can do that. As former first lady Barbara Bush once said, if we have children, they must come first. Our success as a nation and as families depends less on what happens in the White House than what happens in our own homes.[48]

I think Mr. Thomas states it well. We are going to have to spend time with our children! We need to study them and learn their personality traits (their natural responses to the world). We need to see what activities interest them. We need to observe their innate talents and strengths. If you have more than one child, you will quickly see that children are different from each other, and it is impossible to relate to all children in the same way. Proverbs 20:11-12 says that "Even a child is known by his doings, whether his work be pure, and whether it be right. The hearing ear, and the seeing eye, the Lord hath made even both of them." In referring to these verses, Pastor Joe Temple notes:

> These two verses should be read together, connecting the truth of them, which is this: God has given you as parents eyes that can see. He has given you ears that can hear. A child is known by his doings. Watch what he is doing. Listen to what he says. That is the way you will know and understand your child.[49]

I would add here that by watching and listening you will also be able to tell what negative traits, attitudes, and behaviors he has inherited and learned from you. Ouch! Has your child heard you constantly complaining and criticizing? It's likely he will do that too. Has he seen you having fits of temper, disregarding all who may be affected by your anger? Has he seen you worried and fretful over unimportant things? Has he observed your lack of self-control in the areas of overeating, abusing alcohol or drugs, or promiscuity? Watch out! The child will probably imitate all these attitudes and behaviors. One great motivation for changing ourselves is the fact that children do imitate our behaviors. That is why you need to allow God to transform you so that you will have the power to change. By the same token, children will learn positive behavior from their parents. Are you praising your children regularly? Are you complimenting others in their presence? Are you displaying a cooperative attitude with people? Are you encouraging your children in what they desire to do? If you are doing these things, you are equipping your children in a powerful way to deal with whatever life holds in store for them. I believe you can even reverse the effects of prior negative behavior by making a deliberate choice to change. I remember very well one choice I made to change something in my behavior for the sake of my children. I had a critical spirit, which I had picked up from my mother. It was so ingrained I hardly knew I was doing it. However, one day I was confronted by my teenage daughter, who resented my frequent criticism. I was shaken when I came to the realization that I had been unduly criticizing my children for years. When I realized that I was perpetuating a negative, generational "curse," I vowed to change my speaking habits. It took time, but I can say that I have experienced a measure of success in this area.

Another example of someone who has made this kind of positive change that benefited her children was highlighted in a newspaper article entitled, "Alcoholics Victorious." Ponder this story and how the life of Patricia Young might encourage you:

> The main need licking [sic] Patricia Young's heart was to find a way to beat booze and drugs. That would've proven difficult given the circumstances of her life two years ago. Then, she was in Temple, a bartender, still caught up with booze despite a stint with Alcoholics Anonymous.
>
> The day after moving here she knew she was still in trouble with alcohol. That day she wandered into the Family of God Fellowship, a nondescript building downtown. Over time, as she attended church, she started to change. She felt her mind renewing from her experience of God's word, from her daily walk with God. As her spirit became renewed, the need for intoxicants began to diminish, she also realized that if she could be helped with her problem, others could too. [*This led to the forming of the local chapter of Alcoholics Victorious, an organization founded in 1948 in Chicago.*]
>
> At Alcoholics Victorious instead of introducing yourself as an alcoholic, members say that they are a new creation in Christ, and it was her personal relationship with Jesus that seemed to be the element missing from AA meetings. "We emphasize a relationship with the Lord," she said.

> No one is turned away, not even nonbelievers, she said. One of the principles of Alcoholics Victorious is letting nonbelievers attend who are still addicted to alcohol or drugs and who feel compelled to search out the true "higher power"—who the group believes to be Jesus Christ.
>
> That the group, that her faith in God has changed her life is evident. Her concerns have changed from beating her addiction to making amends with her family. She has six children and three grandchildren with whom she wants to make amends. "I want to be alive and see that they grow up."[50]

You can start today to change your own particular curse to blessing. You do not have to remain a "victim," imprisoned by victim thinking. You can change, by daily committing yourself to God and asking for His help. You can be reprogrammed, acting differently by choice. Romans 12:2 says, "Do not conform any longer to the pattern of this world, but be transformed by the renewing of your mind." Our focal text from Psalms 37:27 says, "Turn from evil and do good." Ephesians 6:4 admonishes us as parents: "Fathers, do not exasperate your children; instead, bring them up in the training and instruction of the Lord." Replace those negative words (criticizing, nagging, belittling) with words of blessing. As you absorb the truths of Scripture and start living by scriptural principles, start speaking those truths to your children. Replace bad memories with new, good memories by spending time together.

Family Circle magazine often has good advice for parents, and in the following article it's apparent that the writer must have been influenced by the teachings of Christianity. "Prescriptions for Living," a 1999 article, gives this advice:

> Sometimes it takes adversity to show you that your old

methods of dealing with life just don't cut it. It's at such times that you need to develop new ways of responding. It's possible to survive tough situations—and even turn them to your advantage—merely by acting as if you were the person you wanted to be. When you act like that person, you become that person. The hard part is deciding whom you want to become.

The Power of Love

Does it really matter whether you love people outside your immediate circle? Is there any reason to love your enemies or those who wrong or hurt you? Yes, if you want true peace of mind.

When you choose to love your enemies, they don't exist anymore. Love has a warming effect on even the coldest of hearts. Hatred is bad for the hated and worse for the hater. Love is more powerful and much harder to handle than anger. If that seems like an odd statement, try using love the next time you are in a difficult situation. See how powerful love's effect is on your adversary.

I saw a woman with breast cancer learn about the power of love. She'd grown up in an abusive, alcoholic family and felt bitterness toward her parents. When the young woman developed cancer, she changed her attitude and decided to love her parents in spite of the harm they'd done to her. Her mother moved into her home, and every morning as the woman left for work she would tell her mother she loved her. The mother never answered. One morning, after three months, the daughter was late for work and rushed out of the house. Her mother followed her to the door and yelled out to her, "You forgot something." "What did I forget?" the woman asked. "You forgot to say I love you." The woman returned; they cried, embraced and healed.

> Loving your family can be harder than loving your enemies. You may remember the song with the line, "Accentuate the positive, eliminate the negative." That's a description of how to love your family. Instead of criticizing your child's unhealthy behavior and tell her what she shouldn't do, tell her you love her and you wish she would take good care of the daughter you love, because you don't want anything bad to happen to her.
>
> *Be Thankful for Your Problems*
> Good things can come from adversity. You can learn to be grateful. If your gratitude depends on what life gives you or what other people do for you or to you, you will be disappointed more often than you are grateful. But you can learn to feel more grateful by rethinking your attitude toward life. First, remember that contentment lies in giving. If you know that giving is better than receiving, then you can feel grateful for what you are able to give to others.
>
> Even when you can't change your life any other way, you can still change your attitude. And when you do, your life changes. You find more chances to love, and you will be surprised to see how much more love is returned to you.[51]

From an article in the November, 2000 issue of Good Housekeeping magazine is a section called "Your Kids' Emotional Health." The article is entitled "Give them their vitamins, minerals, & a daily dose of joy." It states:

> As a parent, I have a responsibility to steer my children away from life's perils....But equally important, I think, is helping them savor the small, unexpected moments when joy happens. I want to find a way to foster these moments and encourage my children to

> see them for the gifts they are.
>
> "The joy a child experiences works much like an emotional vaccine," says Arlene Kagle, Ph.D., a psychologist who works with families. "It's something that will protect us later, when we're adults and life throws us the inevitable curve."[52]

In the same issue of Good Housekeeping, Melissa Fay Greene writes "Surprising news about self-esteem:"

> The most reliable path to self-esteem is for a kid to attempt a goal he or she believes is too hard, to work toward it and, finally, either to accomplish it—run the mile, finish the book, write the report—or to feel that a good try was made.
>
> Three ways to give praise that counts:
>
> TAKE YOUR CUES FROM THE CHILD—Don't impose adult values on his or her sense of accomplishment. If the child looks pleased or happy, then it's fine to say, "That was hard," or "Good work."
>
> LEAVE ROOM FOR FURTHER ACHIEVEMENT—If you get to "Spectacular!" right away, you can't backtrack to "Excellent."
>
> SPRINKLE THE CHILD'S DAY WITH NONCONTINGENT COMMENTS SUCH AS "I LOVE YOU" AND "YOU'RE SUCH A GOOD KID"—Not being associated with things done, these go to the essence of the child's sense of self: *I may not always do praiseworthy things, but I—inherently—am a good person.*
>
> Praise is not nearly as useful to a child as the truth.[53]

That last phrase of the quote is worth repeating. *Praise is not nearly as useful to a child as the truth.* I find it interesting that even secular writers recognize the importance of dealing in truth. Of course the Bible strongly urges us to be honest in all our relationships. We're reminded that truth-telling has high value to God. David, as Psalmist, in his penitent prayer of Psalm 51, says to God: "Surely you desire truth in the inner parts" (verse 6). We need to speak the truth to our children—the truth about our past failures—and start living in truth before them. Children seem to instinctively know when we are truthful or not. They are very quick to notice hypocrisy. If we desire to break the cycle of generational sin in our families, we must be honest. Our children's concepts of God as Father depend to a great degree on the kind of parenting they receive from us.

We must consider parenting as our first "ministry of reconciliation" (2 Corinthians 5:18). If we fail here, it is doubtful how effective our other ministries will be. If your children are still young and living at home, you have much opportunity to put into practice not only good parenting skills, but opportunity to influence your children's behavior in the future. They will be better able to avoid the trap of victimization as you allow God to bring healing in your relationship with them. Help them to see that you will not continue a pattern of hurtful behavior, and that they can choose to never start it. Breaking the cycle of hurtful family experiences should be a priority, and it is worth every effort that you can make to accomplish it.

However, you may think that it is too late for your family. Perhaps your children are already teenagers or adults living away from home. Perhaps they have already been victimized by your behavior, and have responded with fear, anger, and bitterness. What can you do now to bring about reconciliation and healing? First, know that it is not too late. I have seen families that have gone through this reconciliation process long after the children have left their parental homes. God is in the business of redemption and reconciliation and He is working in the lives of the individual members of your family. As I have examined my own family experiences, I have seen several major facets of reconciliation at work.

(1) First of all, you need to acknowledge your guilt (to God and to your children). Your children will not be surprised that you have been guilty of some abusive act or attitude! Acknowledging your guilt and confessing the sinfulness of your behavior will be very powerful in bringing down the walls of separation that have risen between you and your children. What could be more disarming? Accepting blame, or responsibility for your actions, is in short supply in the world today. We as Christians can be examples to the world as we do this with our children.

(2) Secondly, and perhaps the most important facet of reconciliation at work, is asking your child for forgiveness. I have already covered the subject of forgiveness at length in previous chapters, so I will not belabor the point here. Just remember, your asking to be forgiven is an act of obedience on your part and does not depend on the other person's response. You are accountable to God to do the right thing. If the other person chooses to forgive you, so much the better for him. Forgiving you will eliminate the reason for his anger and resentment. The kind of forgiveness discussed above takes into account the action of another and helps the wronged person to make a decision to build a new kind of relationship.

(3) Love your children unconditionally. You may see in your grown children some very undesirable traits and evidence that they are perpetuating abusive behavior. They may not even forgive you but rather choose to hold on to bitterness. God's Spirit will enable you to love them anyway. Unconditional love will allow you to value them as people

and enable you to show respect for them just because they are created by God.

(4) After you go through the first three steps of action—acknowledging your guilt; asking for forgiveness; and loving unconditionally—you must commit the other person to the Lord in prayer. Now begins your very important ministry to your child—a lifelong ministry. That is the ministry of prayer. You cannot control their responses, their actions, or their attitudes. You cannot force them to make right choices—choices that will lead to their own freedom and healing. However, you can pray for them. In some cases it may take years for God to accomplish His work of reconciliation in the hearts of your children. But you are called upon to be faithful in prayer for them—persistent, specific, frequent prayer. One of the purposes for Jesus' coming as Messiah to the earth was that He would "turn the hearts of the fathers to their children and the disobedient to the wisdom of the righteous—to make ready a people prepared for the Lord" (Luke 1:17). Your prayers on behalf of your children will help them turn to the Lord, the One who can enable them to become overcomers. They, too, can realize God's healing for their hurts and His purpose for their lives.

We have been called to be ministers of reconciliation, and we have a message of reconciliation. Let us be faithful to this task in our homes first of all, then go out into the world of hurting, dying people who need the great reconciler—Jesus Christ.

Jesus Christ knew what it meant to be a victim. He lived as a human being upon this earth, and although He only did good works, He was unappreciated. In His closing days before the crucifixion, He was mocked, falsely accused, tried unjustly, and betrayed by close friends. He was beaten, spat upon, ridiculed, and hung exposed on a rough wooden cross, with His hands and feet pierced by crude iron nails. He suffered greatly at the hands of cruel, unrepentant men who rejected Him and His message. Yet, He did all this willingly, sacrificially. Why? Because He looked beyond the cross to the victory that lay ahead. He chose to become a victim so that you and I could be reconciled to God. Yes, He would be killed and buried, but He rose again to show the world His power over death and hell. He became the ultimate victim in order to give us the ultimate victory—to all who place our faith in Him to be our Savior. If we have made the choice of committing our lives to God through Jesus Christ, we have His Holy Spirit living within us. This is how we can be victorious. Though we have been victimized, we do not need to live our lives with a "victim" mentality. Romans 12:21 says, "Do not be overcome by evil, but overcome evil with good." And 1 John 5:5 asks and answers the question, "Who is it that overcomes the world? Only he who believes that Jesus Christ is the Son of God." We can be overcomers.

CHAPTER SIXTEEN

Victors' Hall of Fame

By trusting God, we are saying that we have confidence God can bring good out of evil. Even as we look at the worst of circumstances in our lives, if we remain teachable, we will be able to see God at work. He is shaping us into the image of His Son Jesus, which means that we must share in the sufferings of the Savior. In this chapter, I want to share with you the stories of some whom I have interviewed who fought the battles of victimization and have come out on the other side victoriously. The victory was fully experienced when each of these looked back and saw God working through his/her circumstances to ultimately bring good out of evil.

From Overacheiver to Overcomer

I would like to share first the story of Nina*. Nina started her life as a bubbly, vivacious child, but the sexual abuse thrust upon her by a family friend drove her into a shell of silence and pain. Even before the abuse by her "adopted grandfather," she already had a sense of being unwanted in

* Names of these real people have been changed to protect their privacy.

her family of origin. Her father, who was always emotionally, and frequently physically, absent from her, had resented her birth. She got the message that she was the "oops" baby, being the fifth daughter born to a dirt-poor Texas ranching family. Her father was very stern and extremely critical of her.

Her father's disapproval caused her to be drawn to the man next door because initially he offered her acceptance and approval. Acceptance had been a source of affirmation for the two years leading up to the sexual encounter when she was ten. He would even tell her, "I wish my little granddaughter was more like you".

His betrayal of her innocence was such a shock because this once kind, warm, accepting and approving gentleman became angry and physically threatening. The effects of this man's abuse were profound and would impact on who she was becoming and last for many years into adulthood. She expresses in her own words what she felt at the time:

> Was there no one a child could trust? My mother, after several weeks, became so worried about me that she began to question me. "Why don't you go outside and sit on the porch with the neighbors anymore? Why do you sit in the corner and read all the time? Why didn't you want to go to the movies with the neighbors?" She noticed that I would wince when, through the paper-thin walls [of the duplex], I would hear the abuser's voice. Little by little, she began to pull the horrible truth from me. I remember my sobs and crying, "I'm sorry, Mama...I didn't do anything bad, did I?" My mother's response was "You must never tell anyone else about this....If you tell anyone else, we will have to move and there are no other places we can afford to live.... Never, never tell a soul about this!!!!!!...You must promise to keep this a secret."

> When your abuser reminds you not to tell anyone, that this is "just our secret" and no one would understand, you begin to feel a sick-like sensation. When he angrily tells you that he will have to really hurt you if you tell anyone, you, the child, are frightened and yet already there is a sense of shame, guilt, and sinful secrecy that sweeps over you. As a 10-year-old growing up in the late 40's, I had absolutely no knowledge of sex. I thought that the physical pain and danger to me was because my abuser had hatred in his heart toward me. I knew immediately that I had been violated...and was grateful that he had not killed me.

Shame, silence, and secrecy—the three bywords of sexual abuse. How devastating it is for a child to suffer this kind of abuse. So many questions went unanswered:

- What had I done that was so wrong?
- Was my mother punishing me?
- Why???
- Did all men hurt and abandon me?
- Was I dirty?
- Was my abuser going to get me alone again and try to hurt and perhaps kill me?
- Did he do the same acts of sexual abuse with his little granddaughter, my best friend?
- Would my heart always feel wounded?
- My body would heal, but would my soul?

The burden of keeping the secret was almost too much for her, but at least her mother cared for her enough to realize she needed some distance from the perpetrator of the crime. In the summers she would send Nina away to live with an older, married sister so she could baby-sit for her. Although her mother said she was helping the family in this way, Nina just felt as if she were being sent away because she was not wanted by her parents. During the months she did live at home, she was in constant dread of being in the presence of her abuser and even experienced a terrifying chill whenever she heard his voice.

Somehow, Nina found a way of coping. She became an aggressive tomboy, challenging all the boys at school games and even fighting with some of them. She felt she had to prove herself mentally and physically to her world. The only way to do this was to pretend she wasn't afraid and become a fighter. Finally, her family moved away from the duplex when she was thirteen, which helped her to begin to make a break with her past. However, she continued to be a victim of low self-esteem, ever feeling she was not quite good enough.

She carried with her into her teenage years the self-blame that is so typical of children who have been abused. She desperately needed to prove herself worthy. The result was that she became an overachiever, receiving many honors and awards in high school. Unfortunately, her father never recognized these achievements and her mother was always too tired and withdrawn to attend the events in which she was involved. Even when she received a full, four-year scholarship to any university of her choice, her parents were not present at the awards ceremony.

Her loneliness and feelings of low self-worth caused her to become an overeater, finding solace in food—a condition that plagues her even today. She also found some solace in writing sad poetry about "the crying clown," but she could not escape her past nor did she know how to deal with it. Many times she seriously contemplated suicide. She lived in fear of any romantic involvement, thinking only of the pain of a possible sexual encounter. Imagine the great inner conflict she endured—needing and seeking love and acceptance from men, yet being afraid of the only kind of "love" she knew. Her words today are:

> Although the sexual abuse only occurred one time, I was traumatized for 40 years. I carried the shame and sense of guilt until I went into counseling at age 50. Within myself, I felt somehow "at fault" and had spent so much of my life trying to please and appease men.

Even after succeeding in college Nina carried into her first marriage the fears that she had had to deal with all of her life. She still carried the secret and was afraid to tell her husband, thinking that he would reject her. Unable to deal with her husband's anger at times drove her to suicidal thoughts. She often had flashbacks of the abuse scenes from her childhood. To add to her burdens, her husband's family also rejected her. They were blamers and when her second child was born anencephalic, she was blamed because "God was punishing her for not being a better mother!" Again, she went into the state of silent withdrawal, filled with anguish and alienation. One final tragic blow to her faltering self-worth came when her husband, after twenty-five years of marriage, announced he wanted a divorce.

In spite of all this abuse and rejection, Nina today is a very different person from that frightened little girl of ten, the tomboy out-to-prove-it teenager, the young adult bound up with her past. What has made the difference? How has she come to a place of healing and overcoming? Nina came into my life several years ago, and I could see that she had a story to tell—one of God's empowering transformation. So, I asked her about her life. Looking back, she assessed her life and saw the hand of God upon her. She saw how God even began the healing process long before she was totally committed to Him. Her mother had sent her to Sunday School (walking alone for three miles), and even though Nina interpreted this to mean she had sinned and needed to go to church for forgiveness, it was a step that God provided in her healing journey. She says of those years:

> Thank God, I did have a few wonderful Christian teachers and friends who gave me much needed support. It was only the grace of God and the Christian ethics which had been imparted to me that kept me from being extremely promiscuous and another teen pregnancy statistic.

For the one seeking healing it is important to know the kind of people with whom she surrounds herself. Through church attendance and fellowship with Christians, one is exposed to God's Truth and the love and acceptance of people who really care. For Nina, God had early established a spiritual foundation upon which she could build her life. It would be many years before she fully appreciated this fact, but when her marriage fell apart, she came to realize that she could not "fix" her life alone. She realized that, even with all her talents and intellect, she could not achieve a state of acceptance by God or others. First she had to acknowledge her need of God. This opened the door that led to a place of wholeness. Here is her account:

> There was nowhere to go but to God. All my life I had tried to fulfill a man's need. Now, I needed God. For a time, I actually gave up on God, but praise His wonderful love, He never gave up on me. It was only in counseling that I was able to tell the counselor, "I was sexually abused as a child." Then, I could become whole by facing truth and knowing that God understood. Much of my healing has depended upon my being able to forgive as Christ forgives. I feel that the sexually abused child always lives inside the adult survivor. We must be in balance with ourselves and those "significant other persons" so that we do not slip back into our sense of guilt and unworthiness. Male victimizers can spot us and we must have a strong spiritual base of our acceptance, approval, and affirmation in Christ to be VICTORS.

> Learning to forgive my mother and father for not protecting me was possible only when I realized that God had used my secret shame to drive me to success. My overburdened guilt was, by His power, transformed into overachievement. To forgive my abuser—yes, that occurred. He came to me when I was a university student and asked me to forgive him. I, like so many abused children, have been victimized by the society and situation in which I was bound. Only God's love can free us.
>
> The only truly successful method [of freeing myself from my victim status] was on my knees when I accepted that God was approving of me. He was my ever-present Father. His love was unconditional. I did not have to be abused, for I had a great calling to be used in my Father's kingdom. It's an entirely new me: no more secrets; God loves me just as I am; I am His child; forever loved, forever protected. I remind myself of this with every new day, every scripture I read, each prayer I offer. I am His and He is mine!!!
>
> I am a more positive person than I have ever been before. I find such joy in life. I am capable of great love and understanding. I understand the importance of experiencing God in the secrets of our lives. I am learning to accept that God doesn't judge me by the awards and honors of my life, but He looks into my heart. I am grateful that I have gained more than I ever lost.

As you can see, Nina has become victorious, overcoming an abusive past. We can praise God with her that she not only has experienced healing but also is able to help others in their healing journeys. She has a passion for helping young people who are burdened with sexual problems, such as guilt, teen pregnancy, etc., and offers them deep understanding and Christian-based counsel. She is better able to help her sons and grandchildren because of her experiences, and she delights in doing so. She is a lover of life and spreads the joy of her Christ-like attitude to all who cross her path. Finally, she says:

> I am whole, but each day I reaffirm myself in God's healing power. When I think negative thoughts about myself, I reaffirm that I am His child. He can bring back that bubbly, vivacious little girl who can love, trust, laugh, and live to the fullest.

A Search for Peace

Mindy comes from a very dysfunctional family, being the only daughter among five sons. Both parents were alcoholics who abused her mentally and neglected her emotionally. When she was a young child, her father was sent overseas with the army. While he was away, she was aware of the fact that her mother was involved in an adulterous affair. This affair resulted in an unwanted pregnancy, which ended tragically in the loss of the baby. Mindy's not sure if her mother miscarried or had an abortion. Whichever the case, the knowledge of these events was a heavy load for a young girl to carry.

Also, when she was six years old, Mindy was sexually molested by a 20-year-old uncle. This event scarred her for life. In her young mind, she blamed herself and was angry at her oldest brother for not protecting her. At that time she went into denial, giving up the ability to cry. No one was available for her to talk to and she felt she wouldn't be believed even if she told what had happened. She became fearful of relationships and thought that she had no control over what was done to her.

As is true in many such cases of early childhood sexual abuse, Mindy became promiscuous as a teenager. Her promiscuity led to an unwanted pregnancy and her parents pressured her to have an abortion. She refused and chose to give birth to the child and give her up for adoption. By this time in her life, she concluded that sex had no value and she, as a person, had little value as well.

At age sixteen she confronted the uncle that had abused her. He denied that the abuse had ever taken place and made her feel like she was the one in the wrong. Her response to the trauma of sexual abuse was that of anger toward not only her brother but also toward the church (the uncle and grandparents were involved in a church). She sensed that people connected with the church should have high standards of morality, so the hypocrisy she saw in her relatives led her to believe the church was not for her. Her parents, however, sent her to a private Catholic school, where she observed a different kind of Christianity. She was impressed that the nuns seemed to have a peace for which she desperately longed, but she didn't know how to get it for herself.

Mindy never told anybody about what had happened to her, so no one knew her deepest needs. However, from an early age, she instinctively knew that there was a God and that she could talk to Him. Her knowledge of God was very limited, but in spite of this, her grandmother (with whom she lived part of the time) coerced her to respond to an altar call in her church. Her grandmother actually bribed her, offering her $20 if she would "walk the aisle." She was ten or twelve at the time. The action had little real meaning to her, but she did know that it was not a sincere commitment on her part. So by the time she was twelve, she had experienced sexual abuse, verbal and mental abuse, and spiritual abuse. Her only defense was to become unfeeling. This way she would not have to deal with the pain of it all.

Running from the pain led her into four disastrous marriages and divorces. She did not know what she was looking for, but she desperately needed a sense of family and security. From these marriages she bore three daughters. In every case, Mindy's spouses were abusive and controlling and made her feel guilty. Interestingly enough, the four husbands shared a common history. Each had come from a dysfunctional family which the father had abandoned; each was a Vietnam vet; and each had had a mother who forced religion on him. It is easy to see why Mindy responded to all this abuse with a mixture of fear and anger. She had little self-esteem, felt she was to blame for her troubles, felt "dumb" and "stupid," and learned to trust no one. In addition to these gut-level feelings, she gained a great deal of weight and had other physical manifestations of the stress under which she lived.

Mindy kept pursuing peace, but it seemed to elude her. She didn't know where to turn for help except the medical community. This led her to numerous counselors, psychologists, and psychiatrists. However, she did not share her childhood trauma with any of them. Some gave her counsel—such as confronting parents; reliving past events; getting divorced. Some prescribed medication to treat what they thought was manic/depressive disorder. However, there was no medicine that would heal her fractured heart. Her prayers during this time were for God to "fix" her. That's all she knew to pray.

In spite of all the ways she had been victimized, she had an overcoming mindset to some degree. Some of this was due to innate personality traits. She was determined to make a way for herself in the world. She eventually earned a teaching degree and operated a large day-care center. She had a heart for serving others and even went on to earn a nursing degree. It is remarkable that she could accomplish all this in the midst of such suffering. I believe that God knew of her overcoming spirit and He was at work in all her endeavors. He, however, waited for her to come to the point of brokenness before she was ready to receive His peace—the "peace that passeth all understanding" (Philippians 4:7 KJV).

Mindy had been praying to be "fixed" but she finally came to the realization that what she really needed was to be "broken." She had learned early in her life that she would have to have an independent spirit in order to survive in this world. After her fourth divorce and much heartache, she began to realize that she could not live life to its fullest by depending on herself. She wanted out of the terrible downward spiral which characterized her life. She put in place a plan of action. Mindy went to work in a menial job that did not require that she be around people much of the time. Her job was cleaning a convenience store. As she worked night after night, she began to sense God's presence with her. The cleaning of the floors became symbolic of the cleansing she needed within her tortured soul. She sensed that she just needed to wait on God. She instinctively knew that He would bring about the cleansing and, ultimately, the brokenness that would prepare the way for His mighty work of healing in her.

How did she come to healing? God used many tools at His disposal to heal her. He used other people. She was befriended by a Christian woman, who loved her unconditionally and ministered to her freely, helping her in very practical ways. Through this friendship she began to learn to trust for the first time in her life, and also to realize her need for a female friend. With an invitation from this friend, she began to attend a local Baptist church—a very big step for her, having come from a mixed but mostly Catholic background. It was at her friend's church that she, after much thought, prayer, and counsel, committed her life to Jesus Christ. In this commitment, she realized her need to confess sin and come before a merciful God. By putting her trust in Jesus Christ as her Savior and Lord, she then was ready to receive that wonderful peace for which she had sought her whole life (some forty years). As she continued to attend that Baptist church, she began to have a voracious appetite for God's Word. She bought her first Bible, and the words of healing and comfort began to fill the empty places in her soul. Another tool God used to speak to her was Christian music. Many times when the spoken word could not reach her, the lyrics of a song on a well-worn tape would. Mindy was also influenced by different books that carried hopeful messages. The fellowship of Christians with whom she now surrounded herself also played an important role in her achieving victory over her past. Newfound Christian friends prayed for her and with her and loved her like no one had ever loved her. One of these friends, a godly man, ultimately became her husband. Although she is still not sure she is worthy of his love, she knows that he is a gift from God. She knows now that she is no longer alone on her journey through life. She can walk ahead into the future with confidence that not only can she be victorious but she can be used by God to help others find their way to victory as well. The journey, of course, has not ended. There are still times when some need rises to the surface that she has not yet been able to give to God, but she knows that when these needs arise, along with the need comes a confidence that He will meet those needs. She is succeeding in her efforts to rid herself of the emotional baggage and spiritual bondage under which she lived for so long. Mindy now experiences the peace of God and has a great desire to share that peace with others.

Angel Unaware

Victimization does not always come to us at the hands of another person. We can also be victimized by circumstances. To our finite minds, this is difficult to understand, and we can quickly be overwhelmed when things are out of control. There seems to be no way to explain what happens and why it happens. For many that are caught in the circumstances of life, there seems to be no way out. Nor is there much confidence or hope that they will make it through, either.

Christians, however, who are "under the circumstances" of tragedy or trial, can hope that God will "work all things together for good" (Romans 8:28). We need to accept that God has a plan for us and is developing our character through these circumstances that we do not understand. If we have open minds and open hearts we can learn much of value during hard times. This is particularly true for one who has wandered far from God and is trying to live apart from the reality that we are all accountable to God.

My next victory story illustrates in a graphic way how God sometimes uses extreme circumstances to get our attention and put us back on track, following His will for our lives. Let me introduce you to Carl, who had a very dramatic encounter with God that changed his life completely. I will let Carl tell his own story, as he told it to me.

> On March 9, 1996 I was driving a truck from Houston to Missouri, and I wanted to stop in Corrigan, Texas to visit my mother. Two weeks prior to this day my grandfather had died and I couldn't go to the funeral, so I decided to stop and visit my mother and grieve with her. I arrived in Corrigan around 6 p.m. on Friday. It was about 25 degrees or so when I stopped at a truck stop and unhooked my trailer. I drove on out in my truck alone to where I thought my mother lived. I had only been out there one other time. I turned, and I realized I was lost. In the process of getting lost, I turned down several different roads, and wound up turning down a dead-end road.
>
> At the end of this dirt road there was a deer camp that had a wide spot where I could turn around. So I started to turn around, and I got stuck in some soft dirt. I must have tried for about 30 to 45 minutes to get the truck unstuck. I used regular means, which was to back up and pull forward, but the truck wasn't going anywhere. So, I decided to get out and start putting things under

the tires. Over at the deer camp there were boards, so I got them from there and put some under the tires.

I got back into the truck, put it into gear, and tried to pull off. That wasn't working. It just spit everything out the back. So, I looked around for a pretty good-sized limb or log. I found a log about 6 inches in diameter, and about 4 feet long. I rolled it to where it laid in front of the tires. I got back in the truck and put it into gear. It was spinning on the log and was not catching. I went back there and kicked the log once while the truck was still in gear. I kicked the log once more, and it wouldn't work. I kicked it again, and that is when my leg was pulled under the tire. The tires were spinning on me. They must have been spinning for about 90 seconds. All during that time, I was screaming and crying and calling on Jesus. After about 90 seconds, the tire stopped.

During this time my leg was torn up very badly. There was a lot of damage. The wounds were being cauterized at the same time they were created, so I did not lose a lot of blood (actually about a pint). My clothes were literally ripped off. Again, it was only about 25 degrees out there. The reason the tires stopped, I was told later by a mechanic, was because a computer inside made the truck quit. I believe that the computer might have turned it off, but I believe in my heart that the Lord helped do that. I was screaming and asking Him to stop the tires from spinning and they did. When that happened, I just kind of lay back and tried to catch my breath, wondering what I was going to do. I was still crying out in panic. I decided I wasn't going to accomplish anything by freaking out, so I started to calm down. I started praying out loud to God. I asked Him to save me because this was no place to die: not on the cold, hard ground alone like this. He gave me a sense of peace, and I made my peace with Him then. I sat up and started trying to pull myself out of there. It wasn't working. Every time I would pull on my leg it felt as though it was being pulled out of the socket. It kept swelling, and every time I would pull it, it would swell more. So, I just lay back down and said, "Lord, I need your help. I need you to pull me out from here so I will not freeze to death. Please help!!!" He came and put His hands on my shoulders as plain as day, and it scared me. I turned my head around to look, and there wasn't anybody there, but I could still feel those hands right on my shoulders. I said, "Thank you for coming, Lord, and I praise you for this. I need your help bad." No sooner had I said this than I put my hands down on the injured leg and I felt God's hands roll down my arms and come right on top of my hands. Then we gave a solid pull, and the leg came right out. Like I said, I had been trying unsuccessfully for two hours to get this leg out, but it came right out with the help of the Lord. All I had to do was call and ask Him.

I was lying there and just praising Him for this. I don't know if this was a physical being that came and helped me. I could not see it, but I could feel it. I don't know if it ever left, but I started having a conversation, a prayer conversation, with this being. I was convinced that it was God; no other being in the world could match this power that I felt around me. I started thanking Him and praising Him. I told Him right then and there that I was going to do His work the rest of my breathing life if I lived past this. I hadn't been really close to God before this happened. I was saved, but had fallen away. I had lived in the world, but decided right then and there that the world didn't have anything I ever needed. I started serving God right then.

He gave me the energy to get back into the truck. I crawled and got back into the truck and turned the engine back on and the heater. I crawled under a blanket and everything I had to try to warm up my body because I was going into shock. I was just lying there. It was about 10:45-11:00 p.m. when I got back into my truck. I called on the CB, but I couldn't reach anybody. I could hear somebody in the background, but they couldn't hear me. I was calling and honking my horn, but I knew the horn wasn't going to do me any good because the nearest house was 6 miles away. So, I just lay down and started talking to God again. I was begging God to let me live a couple of more days so I could say good-bye to my family and tell them that I was going to be okay. As I was lying there, I started to feel sleepy. I know it was probably a sign of shock. I started to fall asleep, and then I started to see this bright white light. Then my spirit started to come up out of my body (I was facing down at the time), and I was looking at my body. I started to rise up towards this bright white light, and I went through the top of my truck. I saw insulation and wiring and everything as I passed through the top. As I started going toward this bright light, I just kept on going and going and going. I got to the bright white light, and all of a sudden it was like I had landed on top of a cloud.

It took me a few minutes to realize that I was actually walking through this place. I looked down and there wasn't any damage to my leg. I was completely whole, and it felt just wonderful. I was walking toward this deep bright light that was at the back side of wherever I was. All around me there were no shadows, and it was kind of like being on a cloud. As I started walking again, I saw all of these figures coming to me. The first figure I came to was my grandmother on my mother's side. She died when I was six years old. When I looked at her face, I knew exactly who she was, even though I had never seen even a picture of her when she was young. Here, she looked like she was about 16. She had a beautiful face and long flowing hair, and her hands were outstretched. She was smiling at me. Like I said, I had never seen a picture of her like this. The pictures I had seen of her were taken when she was old. She didn't say anything, and I couldn't speak, although I tried. She was just smiling at me and had her hands out. The next one I passed was my grandfather who had just died. He too looked like he was about 16, just perfect in body and spirit. Next, along came my Uncle Robert, who had died in 1959, ten years before I was born. He was beautiful, too. It seemed like Heaven to me, or what I had always thought Heaven might be.

I kept passing people, ancestors probably. There were some of them that I didn't recognize. There were some that had died 50 years before I was born. They knew me, but there were just a few that I recognized. I kept going, and all of a sudden I started sliding backwards. I wasn't falling, just sliding backwards. I passed everybody again, a little faster this time. I was trying to grab at everything, trying to stay. I didn't want to leave. I fell back down, and watched as the light faded away. I fell back through the truck and saw the wiring, insulation and all. I went back into my body. It seemed like about 5 minutes after I fell into the dash of my truck, and it was 7:30 a.m. When I had fallen asleep it was 11:30 p.m. I believe in my heart that the Lord made my physical body die so I could be found later, and to be able to tell this story of how beautiful Heaven is, and what we have in store for us if we give our hearts to the Lord. When I woke up I just felt renewed, and I had a new energy. Something went through me and told me to get out and try to find a main road. The main road was about 150 yards away. I needed to crawl all of the way out there. I got down out of my truck, which was a struggle. I must have fallen out, I think. I had to crawl around to the front and start toward that road. I got to the middle of the road. I looked around for a minute trying to clear my vision. I looked outside, and it was daylight. I looked at the clock on the dashboard, and it was 7:30 a.m. Then came a white Chevrolet. I thought that I was dreaming when this truck drove up. But it did! It was a white Chevrolet pickup with two young men in the truck. I was dying of thirst, and one of the guys had a little bit of Dr. Pepper. They gave me the Dr. Pepper and I drank it. it. It wet my mouth so I could talk. I told them what had happened, and I told them how sick and bad I felt. They called 911 for an ambulance in Diboll, Texas, which was up the road from Corrigan. They took me to Diboll, and we met the ambulance. From there I was taken to a hospital in Lufkin. I was there about three hours when my parents showed up. The doctors had told my mother out in the waiting area that I probably wouldn't make it to Galveston. They were going to send me to Galveston to the burn hospital. The doctor said that poisons in my leg were cutting everything off and affecting my heart and other parts of me. My mother and step-father came in and started talking to me in the emergency room. I told them right there, "If I don't make it, I'll see you in Heaven because I have gone there already. I made peace with God and that's where I am going to go." I know Mother broke down, but she didn't show it to me. She didn't want to upset me anymore than I already was. I told both of them that I loved them. I was on the way out of the emergency room on the gurney going to the Life Flight Helicopter. Momma walked out with me, and I told her one more time that I loved her. I said, "If I don't see you again, then I will see you in Eternity." We took off, and I probably remember about 20 minutes of the flight. I started to choke, and my breathing became really low. I was fully unconscious. They said when I got to the helicopter pad at John Sealy Hospital they were doing CPR trying to keep my heart beating. When my parents arrived about two hours later, the surgeons had already taken my leg off up above my knee. The doctors told my parents that they were going to try to stabilize me with that much leg left. I didn't stabilize but just kept getting worse. Because of this, the doctors had to remove more of my leg, leaving me just six inches of leg. This was the only way they could stop the poison that was going into my body.

After two days I finally began to stabilize, but had a lot of ups and downs. Early on in this life-and-death struggle, Mother called every church in the yellow pages, asking them to pray for me. I tell you, prayer works! The doctors worked on me a few days later for about seventeen hours, and I died again, on the table. They finally came out and told my mother that they only had one thing left to offer me—dialysis. They told me that my kidneys were completely gone and they would probably have to take them out or I would have dialysis for the rest of my life. They did dialysis and started removing fluid off my body. I had swollen to about twice my normal size, weighing about 400 pounds. The fluid started coming off, and my mother said that they probably drained off about 2-5 gallons of fluid. They said it was like 90-weight oil. It actually wore out the dialysis machine trying to pump all that out of me. About seven days later they told my mom that if I lived seven days they would give me a 50% chance of survival.

I lived seven more days, but my lungs filled up with fluid. I was drowning in my own fluid, and my heart started quivering. I could tell that people were still praying for me. Even though I was still unconscious, I could still feel the presence of the Lord in my room. After a few more days, the doctors came in and noticed that there was a little bit of yellow fluid in the urine bag, demonstrating that my kidneys were beginning to function again. The doctors were amazed. In another

> few days, I started breathing on my own, and a couple of days after that I woke up and found out that I had been unconscious for eighteen days! I started asking for people, and a string of visitors came pouring in to see me. Every day I would improve more, and the doctors told my parents that it would be three to six months before I could leave the hospital. About 28 days later, however, I rolled out of there in a wheelchair. I praise the Lord for it.
>
> I want to tell anyone who reads this that no matter how hard your life gets, no matter what you go through, God will always be there. But it is up to you. You have to ask Him to come into your life. He gives you a choice. If you don't choose Him, you are bound for Hell. I give you this truth. Don't let something like my experience take place in your life before you get back into God's will. If I had to do it over again, I would have been serving God all along. He sent me back here to earth to spread the Good News about Jesus, what He can do, and what miracles He can perform. Even though the miracles are big and vast in my life, there is one greater miracle I can say is better. I would trade all of the other miracles for this one—that Jesus saved me and that I believe in the Lord and that I love Him.

Carl's story is remarkable, isn't it? Can you imagine going through what he did? What would be your choices in the midst of such trauma. You see, Carl had choices to make all along the way. He could have responded very differently to this particular set of circumstances. He was caught in a situation he didn't choose and over which he had no control. He could have given way to his fears and given up any attempt to free himself from his dilemma. Instead, he courageously endured. I believe he was able to do this because he had called upon God to help him. God not only freed him physically from the grip of the truck's tire, but He also freed him from captivity to his fear. He was able to call upon God, expecting Him to help, because He had already established a relationship with Him by professing his faith in Christ.

Carl could have chosen to be angry, blaming God for his getting lost and finding himsclf in this predicament. Anger would not have freed him, however. Many people lash out at God when things don't go their way. Was God to blame? Did God cause this accident? Carl could have questioned God—why? Carl could have felt sorry for himself, thinking that the world was against him. He could have taken credit for his survival, thinking he had done it on his own.

In the crucial moment, however, Carl made the right choice—calling on God. This was the best choice he could make—recognizing his need and powerlessness, and looking to God, his only hope. During this encounter with God, Carl also recognized his need for repentance. Remember, he said he had drifted from the Lord, and knew he needed to be living for God. He saw his sinfulness and asked for forgiveness and committed himself to serving God in the future.

Carl has followed through on the commitment he made to God during those trying hours. I met Carl in 1999 and was delighted in his enthusiastic testimony of how God had worked in his life. He has a great heart of compassion for people who have lost their way and eagerly shares with them how they can be saved. Today he walks on one leg, with the aid of crutches, but he is whole and complete in his inner self because He has placed his faith in Christ. God is using his trauma for good. Just as Carl said, his triumph was a miracle, but a greater miracle is that the God of the universe loves us and chooses to use us to be a blessing to others.

The choices we make in response to victimization have far-reaching results. By our attitude we can curse others or bless others. This truth can be seen in our children. It is so easy for children to pick up attitudes from their parents. If a person responds in anger and does not deal with that anger, his/her children are likely to have a problem with anger. The same is true of fear. When we consider how powerfully we influence our children, we should be greatly motivated to be overcomers. The following story involves a mother and her response to her son's being victimized. What mother does not rise up in defense of her child when she senses there is a threat?

A Mother's Love

Melanie is a single mom, and doing the best she can to bring up her son. I do not know much about her former husband, but it is obvious he came from a dysfunctional family. Though Melanie has divorced him, she still has had to maintain ties with his family for the sake of her son who needs to have a relationship with his grandparents. His father also has visitation rights, so his son Timmy has much exposure to this family. An incident happened when Timmy was eight that had the potential for long-term anger and fear to set in.

Melanie shared with me what happened. On one of his visits with his father, Timmy's uncle molested him. Unlike many abused children who never tell anyone about this kind of thing, Timmy did tell his mother. She could see that he was very upset and distant on his return home. So she coaxed him to tell her what had happened. When she learned that her son had been violated, she became extremely angry. She confesses she had thoughts of violence toward the perpetrator. All of her instinctive sense of protectiveness rose up and she wanted to see the uncle punished for harming her son. Her anger did not last, though. She also had a great concern for this family because she could see that abusive behavior was passed on to the children. She determined that she would do whatever it took to put the cycle to an end as far as her child was concerned. Timmy was a victim in this scenario, but so was Melanie. Initially, she felt "out of control" and unable to change the past. However, she took steps of action that would help her son deal with the incident and hopefully help prevent future encounters like the one that had traumatized him. She knew that she could not make the uncle change, but she knew she could change because she is a committed Christian.

The steps of action that Melanie took were primarily prayer and getting Christian counseling. These were what got her through this difficult time of dealing with her son's fear and her anger. Through prayer she was able to forgive the uncle and receiving counsel gave her and Timmy a way to work through all the emotional ups and downs. Both mother and son were able to talk openly and honestly about what had happened, and this was very healthy. She has also experienced the prayer support of friends. The results of prayer, counseling, and support from others have been very positive for her and her son. There will be long-term ramifications to arise out of the abuse, just as in any sinful behavior there are long-term consequences. Timmy cannot see his grandmother or uncle (the grandmother sided with her son), so those relationships were very affected. It may take a while for Timmy to be able to fully trust again, but he is well on his way to emotional health because of his mother's sensitivity.

Melanie serves as a good role model in how to come to terms with anger toward an abuser. Yes, she was angry, but she allowed God to work in her heart, enabling her to forgive the offender. What a wonderful example to set for her son! Timmy will probably be saved from a lifetime of deep-seated bitterness because his mother cared enough to help him and was even willing to give up her "right" to be angry. Melanie was able to do this because she has turned everything over to God, and as one of God's obedient children she will be blessed for her faithfulness. I close this story with Melanie's own words: "I have learned to forgive in my heart, and I can talk about it [the abuse] more easily. I don't get as emotional as I used to. I certainly do not get as angry. I'm thankful for the Lord."

Let us be encouraged in our own struggles as we read of others' victories. Let us also realize that victory comes to those who make the right choices. God has promised us who believe and trust in Him that we can be overcomers. In one of the epistles of Saint John, he expresses his concern that those early Christians would be overwhelmed by the trials they were suffering. He knows that immature Christians can be easily led astray by false doctrine and false prophets (1 John 4). These false doctrines are still alive today. Beware, because they offer counterfeit victory—victory that does not last but only gives temporary relief. We have seen how the "patterns" of worldly thinking need to be avoided. Let us recognize and proclaim that real victory only comes from God. John, in his first epistle, encourages through these words: "You, dear children, are from God and have overcome them [false prophets], because the one who is in you is greater than the one who is in the world." And 1 John 5:3-4 says:

> This is love for God: to obey his commands. And his commands are not burdensome, for everyone born of God overcomes the world. This is the victory that has overcome the world, even our faith. Who is it that overcomes the world? Only he who believes that Jesus is the Son of God.

We are further encouraged by these passages:

> No, in all these things we are more than conquerors through him who loved us. I am convinced that neither death nor life, neither angels nor demons, neither the present nor the future, nor any powers, neither height nor depth, nor anything else in all creation, will be able

> to separate us from the love of God that is in Christ Jesus our Lord. (Romans 8:37-38)

> His divine power has given us everything we need for life and godliness through our knowledge of him who called us by his own glory and goodness. Through these he has given us his very great and precious promises, so that through them you may participate in the divine nature and escape the corruption in the world caused by evil desires. (2 Peter 1:3-4)

These are strong words of encouragement coming from the Creator Himself. God gives us words of life and we need to pay attention. With the knowledge that we have gained from examining Scripture, let us move on and determine in our hearts that we will do things differently for the sake of the generations to come. The real possibility of healing is ours. Where are you in your journey to healing? Perhaps you have already experienced God's remedy for those who have been poisoned by a lifetime of fear or anger. If you have, you need to realize that the healing is not the ultimate goal, but rather a major step on the way to becoming a child of God who is participating in His Kingdom work. God has a plan that spans the past and the future. He does care about us as individuals and has a plan for each person who has placed his faith in Jesus Christ. His plan takes us past our own experiences and into the future as we influence our children and grandchildren. Christianity is a religion of hope—giving the promise that there is a way of living that is better than what the world has to offer. We can and must offer this hope to our children, so they are not poisoned by the chronic fear, anger, and bitterness that have characterized our lives. If we are free from our past bondage, then we are free to change the way we live life. Victim or victor? The choice is yours.

Notes

Chapter Two

[1] Douglas Weiss, Recovery Works Addiction Symposium report, *Temple Daily Telegram*, (March 29, 1996).

[2] Frank, Jan, A Door of Hope, (San Bernadino, CA; Here's Life publishers, 1987), p. 16.

[3] (Frank, p. 31).

[4] (Frank, p. 34).

[5] (Frank, p. 63).

[6] (Frank, p. 16).

[7] (Frank, p. 63).

[8] "Justice paints bleak picture of jail inmates." *Temple Daily Telegram, (*April 27, 1998).

[9] Ibid.

[10] "Straying husbands, lovers spread cervical cancer" *Temple Daily Telegram, (*August 7, 1996).

[11] Dr. Henry Brandt & Kerry L. Skinner, The Heart of the Problem, (Nashville, TN: Broadman & Holman Publishers, 1995), p. 5.

[12] (Frank, p. 91).

Chapter Three

[13] R.C. Sproul, Ligonier Ministries, Orlando, Florida.

Chapter Four

[14] (Frank, p. 79).

[15] (Weiss, *Temple Daily Telgram,* March 29, 1996).

[16] "Janet Dailey, romance novelist, apologizes for plagiarizing books," *Temple Daily Telegram,* (July 31, 1997).

[17] "ADA affording rights to the obnoxious?" *Temple Daily Telegram,*(April 4, 1996).

Chapter Nine

[18] "Anger in older men raises coronary heart disease risk," *Temple Daily Telegram,* (November 1, 1996).

[19] "Foot-Binding Custom Causes Disabilities in Chinese Women," *Doctor's Guide to Medical and Other News* (Website).

Chapter Ten

[20] "How Love Heals." Love & survival: The Scientific Basis for The Healing Power of Intimacy, (New York, NY; HarperCollins Publishers, 1998.).

[21] (Brandt, p. 53).

[22] Unger, Merrill F. 1961.Chicago: Moody Press.

[23] "Forgiving those who hurt you." Baptist Standard, November 15, 1995.

[24] Ibid.

[25] ten Boom, Corrie, Jesus is Victor, (Michigan: Fleming H. Revell, 1985), p. 26.

Chapter Eleven

[26] Schlessinger, Dr. Laura, "How Could You Do That?!: The Abdication of Character, Courage, and Conscience," (NewYork, NY: Harpercollins Publishers, 1996).

[27] "Reader: girls not only ones molested." Ann Landers column, *Temple Daily Telegram*, (August 7, 1996).

[28] Lucado, Max. 1996. Thomas Nelson Word.

Chapter Thirteen

[29] ("Justice," *Temple Daily Telegram,* March 29, 1996).

[30] Sterling, Beth, The Thorn of Sexual Abuse, (Grand Rapids, Michigan; Fleming H. Revell, 1994.).

[31] "Check early warning signs for abusive behavior in significant other." Ann Landers column, *Temple Daily Telegram,* (June 30, 1997).

[32] (Sterling, p. 82).

[33] "Life Without Father." Reader's Digest, February, 1997.

[34] (Sterling, p. 111).

[35] (Brandt, p. 85).

[36] (Sterling, p. 80).

[37] (Brandt, p. 85).

[38] Blue, Ken, *Healing Spiritual Abuse*, (Downers Grove, Illinois: Intervarsity Press, 1993, p. 14).

[39] Ibid.

[40] (Blue, p. 30).

[41] (Blue, p. 110).

Chapter Fourteen

[42] (Lucado).

Chapter Fifteen

[43] "The best gift" by Tanya Cunningham. *Temple Daily Telegram*, (January 18, 1998).

[44] "Hug your children with positive words" by Ilene Miller. *Temple Daily Telegram*, (April 15, 1998).

[45] "Drugs not always solution for behavior" by George F. Will. *Temple Daily Telegram*, (December 2, 1999).

[46] "Child abuse program presented." *Temple Daily Telegram*, (April 25, 1999).

[47] "Child abuse hitting closer to home in Texas" by Scott Collins. *Baptist Standard*, (April 3, 2000).

[48] "Stop school shooting: Put children first" by Cal Thomas. *Temple Daily Telegram*, (March 30, 2001).

[49] Temple, Joe, Know Your Child, (Grand Rapids, Michigan, Baker Book House Company, 1974.).

[50] "Alcoholics Victorious." *Temple Daily Telegram.*

[51] "Prescriptions for living" by Bernie S. Siegel, M.D. *Good Housekeeping*, (February, 1999).

[52] "Give them their vitamins, minerals & a daily dose of joy" by Joanne Kaufman. *Good Housekeeping*,

(November, 2000).

[53] "Surprising news about self-esteem" by Melissa Fay Greene. *Good Housekeeping*, (November, 2000).

Printed in the United States
1288700002B/139-153

9 781591 601319